The Astonishing
Power of
Emotions

Other Hay House Titles by Esther and Jerry Hicks

(The Teachings of Abraham®)

Books, Calendar, and Card Decks

The Law of Attraction (also available in Spanish)

The Amazing Power of Deliberate Intent (also available in Spanish)

Ask and It Is Given (also available in Spanish)

Ask and It Is Given Cards

Ask and It Is Given Perpetual Flip Calendar

The Law of Attraction Cards

Health, and the Law of Attraction Cards

Manifest Your Desires

Money, and the Law of Attraction (book; CD program; card deck)

Sara, Book 1: Sara Learns the Secret about the Law of Attraction

Sara, Book 2: Solomon's Fine Featherless Friends

Sara, Book 3: A Talking Owl Is Worth a Thousand Words!

The Teachings of Abraham Well-Being Cards

The Vortex (book and CD program)

Getting into the Vortex Meditations (book-with-CD)

Additional CD Programs

The Teachings of Abraham Master Course Audio (11-CD set)

The Law of Attraction (4-CD set)

The Law of Attraction Directly from Source (1 CD)

The Amazing Power of Deliberate Intent (Parts I and II: two 4-CD sets)

Ask and It Is Given (Parts I and II: two 4-CD sets)

Ask and It Is Given: An Introduction to The Teachings of Abraham-Hicks (4-CD set)

The Astonishing Power of Emotions (8-CD set)

Sara, Books 1, 2, 3 (unabridged audio books; 3-CD sets)

DVD Programs

The Law of Attraction in Action, Episodes I–XII (2-DVD sets)

The Teachings of Abraham Master Course Video (5-DVD set)

Think and Get Slim: Natural Weight Loss (2-DVD set)

Ask and It Is Given: An Introduction to The Teachings of Abraham-Hicks (4-DVD set)

❧ 𝕾 ❧

Please visit Hay House USA: **www.hayhouse.com**®;
Hay House Australia: **www.hayhouse.com.au**;
Hay House UK: **www.hayhouse.co.uk**;
Hay House India: **www.hayhouse.co.in**

The Astonishing
Power of
Emotions

Let Your Feelings Be Your Guide

ESTHER AND JERRY HICKS

(The Teachings of Abraham®)

HAY HOUSE, INC.
Carlsbad, California • New York City
London • Sydney • New Delhi

Published in the United States by: Hay House, Inc.: www.hayhouse.com
Published in Australia by: Hay House Australia Pty. Ltd.: www.hayhouse.com.au
Published in the United Kingdom by: Hay House UK, Ltd.: www.hayhouse.co.uk
Published in India by: Hay House Publishers India: www.hayhouse.co.in

Design: Riann Bender

Library of Congress Cataloging-in-Publication Data for the Original Edition

Abraham (Spirit)
  The astonishing power of emotions : let your feeling be your guide / [translated by] Esther and Jerry Hicks. -- 1st ed.
    p. cm.
  "The teachings of Abraham."
  ISBN 978-1-4019-1245-1 (hardcover) -- ISBN 978-1-4019-1246-8 (tradepaper)   1. Spirit writing. I. Hicks, Esther. II. Hicks, Jerry. III. Title.
BF1301.A172 2007
133.9'3--dc22
                              2007012343

Hardcover ISBN: 978-1-4019-1245-1
Tradepaper ISBN: 978-1-4019-6016-2
E-book ISBN: 978-1-4019-2055-5

10 9 8 7 6 5 4 3 2 1
1st edition, September 2007
2nd edition, September 2008
3rd edition, January 2020

Printed in the United States of America

-·:[◙]:·-

We have had the pleasure of meeting with some of the most influential people of our time, and we know of no one person who is more of a fountainhead for the outpouring of positive upliftment than Louise Hay (Lulu), the founder of Hay House—for guided by Lulu's vision, Hay House, Inc., has now become the world's largest disseminator of spiritual and self-improvement materials.

And so, to Louise Hay—and to each person she has attracted to her vision—we lovingly, and with much appreciation, dedicate this book.

-·:[◙]:·-

Contents

Preface

by Jerry Hicks

"This is a great book! . . . For anyone who wants to know how to make their life work better—this is a great book!" That was Esther's exclamation a moment ago while she was evaluating the finishing touches on this, our latest Abraham book, *The Astonishing Power of Emotions*. Esther and I have been writing and publishing books as a husband-and-wife team for two decades, and this is the first time she has *told* me that "this is a great book!" instead of *asking* me, "What do you think of it?"

In my opinion, this is the most innovative and powerful of the series of Abraham books that we have published up to this date. And so, perhaps there will be some readers who will feel that this work is overly complicated, or too Leading Edge for them to grasp. But on the other hand, there will likely be those who will feel that the information is overly simplified or maybe even inappropriate.

My intent in writing this Preface is to guide you around any feeling of *It's too complicated* or *It's too simple* to an awareness that *This is practical, Leading Edge information that you can immediately put to use in order to create more of what you want, or in order for you to be of more value to others.*

Now, what if someone told you that you *do* have a purpose in this life, and that your purpose is that of allowing more joy? And what if someone told you that the true measure of your success in life is your joy?

What if you were told that the inherent basis of your life is freedom, and that not only were you *born* free, but because you have the freedom to choose your own thoughts, you always *are* free?

What if it was explained to you that every time you reach for a thought that makes you feel better, you are, in that moment, achieving your purpose? You are adding to the improvement, to the evolution, of the Well-Being of *All-That-Is*.

What if you were informed that your seemingly solid beliefs are merely the coagulation of a series of individual thoughts that you had at one time thought and then continued to think? What if you were told that from the moment of your birth (and even before), your thoughts, and therefore the formation of your beliefs, were largely influenced by those who came before you?

And what if you were also told that the experiences of your life are, in essence, the result of your dominant thoughts, and that the essence of the thoughts that you focus your attention on long enough becomes manifested into your reality? In other words, "That which I feared has befallen me"; "It is done unto you as you believe"; "Think and grow rich"; "Birds of a feather flock together"; "As ye sow, so shall ye reap. . . ."

So now, consider this: If you had somehow been made aware of the preceding concepts, wouldn't you now want to personally test their validity? Wouldn't there be some points that you would want to clarify for yourself? Would you not, perhaps, feel inspired to take some form of practical action?

Some of you, as you just now read those words, felt them reach back into a place within you where you, at one time, remembered all of this. And if that was the case for you, you may be one who is ready to immediately begin to use this book to refresh your mind regarding not only *who-you-really-are*, but also regarding the value and purpose of your life experience in this current time and place.

That which you call your *conscience* is your imbued belief (fostered upon you by those who came before you) in that which is *right* versus that which is *wrong* for you to be, do, or have. And because this belief system has been imposed upon you from the outside, it can also be modified by the decree of whoever is currently influencing your thoughts.

In other words, our diverse and flexible consciences have been molded by the fears, praise, admonitions, and promised rewards or threatened punishments to be administered (either now or later) by those generations who have come before us. And so, in order to attempt to soothe the consciences of those who, in their fear, seek to control others, each new generation is instructed (even by the famous cartoon character Jiminy Cricket) to "let your conscience be your guide."

Because millions of previous cultures, societies, religions, rulers, leaders, and teachers (and parents, too) have been attempting to pass most of their belief systems on to each newest generation, we find ourselves sharing a world in which there is a wide range of conflicting opinions—as well as violent warfare—relative to *whose* conscience we should allow ourselves to be guided by. In other words, which thoughts, beliefs, or conscience should be your guide as to that which is right or wrong for you?

So, would this not be an appropriate question to ask yourself: *Whose thoughts, beliefs, or ingrained conscience should be my guide as to what is right for me?* Well, this book—with its subtitle, *Let Your Feelings Be Your Guide*—is being given to you in answer to that specific question. *If my purpose is to discover ways to improve the way I feel . . . and if my thoughts equal my beliefs, equal my feelings, and thereby equal my experience . . . and if I can, by the <u>Law of Attraction</u> (the essence of that which is like unto itself, is drawn) change my experience by changing my thoughts . . . then how can I ascertain which of my thoughts/beliefs will ultimately attract that which will ultimately please me?*

This book is unique in many respects, but mainly in that it was written to answer that very question. And the answer, in brief, is: *I'll let my <u>feelings</u> be my guide.*

This work has been written in answer to *your* asking for more. It's not about trying to fix or save a world that doesn't want or need to be fixed or saved (it isn't broken). *These Teachings of Abraham are simply about you continuing to create the joyous, fulfilling life that you have intended to create, while allowing all others to create as <u>they</u> intend.*

You, no matter how wonderful you now feel, you want more. Regardless of how good you feel, you want to feel better. That's the mantra of the ever-expanding Universe: *More! More! More! More expansion. More expression. More exposure. More desire. More life!*

Our planet Earth is populated by billions of us, each asking for an improved life, each asking for a way to feel better than we are now feeling. You and I, individually, have the option in every moment to *allow* ourselves to receive the Well-Being that is natural to us—or to *resist* it. And, in like manner, the billions of others who are also asking for more have that same option. And while there is nothing that we can desire that our abundant, unlimited Universe doesn't have the capacity to give, we cannot receive that which we do not allow.

This book is meant to stand on its own as another comprehensive volume of the Teachings of Abraham. However, it does rest firmly on the shoulders of the accumulated answers to the thousands of questions that so many of us have been asking of Abraham since they began communication with us in 1985.

So, who *is* Abraham? I would describe them as an ineffable Non-Physical phenomenon. I experience them as a "group" of extremely wise and unconditionally loving teachers of practical uses of the natural *Laws of the Universe.* . . . I have described them as the purest form of love I have ever encountered.

Abraham, in some manner, projects blocks of thought (not words) that Esther, my wife, somehow receives (similar to a radio receiver) in answer to our questions. (They never impose themselves on us—they only come when asked for.)

Much as an interpreter might translate a Spanish conversation into English (thought for thought, but not word for word), Esther instantly converts the nonverbal thoughts projected by Abraham into English, Esther's native language. And while I don't understand precisely how Esther is able to do that, I do know that for more than 20 years, I have loved every minute of it . . . because not only has it been personally fulfilling, but I have also had the ongoing pleasure of witnessing Abraham's value to the thousands of you who have been asking the questions that they have been answering.

At the heart of these teachings, from the beginning of our interaction with them, was Abraham's discussion of the Universal *Law of Attraction.* (If you would like a wealth of free information regarding the *Law of Attraction* or the Teachings of Abraham, visit our interactive Website at **www.abraham-hicks.com**.)

In 1985, as this phenomenon began, I asked Abraham for the *Laws of the Universe* by which we could most naturally live our lives (as opposed to the unnatural laws that have been invented by humans as a means to control or inhibit other humans). The first *Law* that Abraham gave us was the *Law of Attraction (the essence of that which is like unto itself, is drawn)*. I don't recall having been aware of the term before Abraham (although as I write this today, there seem to be very few in the English-speaking world who have not recently heard of the *Law of Attraction*). But with the clarity that Abraham focused on it back then, it was new and exciting to me. And so, in 1985, I began to create a series of 20 *Special Subjects* cassette recordings of me asking questions of Abraham regarding ways to improve various aspects of our lives.

Our first recording was entitled *The Law of Attraction,* and that information has now been available for about 20 years—initially in the form of a free introductory recording, and then, also, as a free download on our Website. (Recently we transcribed the first 5 of those 20 recordings and converted them into the first [Hay House, 2006] of what is to be a series of four *Law of Attraction* books): *The Law of Attraction: The Basics of the Teachings of Abraham; Relationships, and the Law of Attraction; Money, and the Law of Attraction;* and *Spirituality, and the Law of Attraction.*

During the subsequent two decades, many authors, screenwriters, and filmmakers (often they belonged to our *Weekly Subscription Program*), sensing the uniqueness, power, and value of Abraham's perspective of life and of the natural *Laws of the Universe*—especially the term *Law of Attraction*—began utilizing the Abraham materials in their many projects. They changed the words slightly and published this information under their own names (occasionally with a reference to where they found the information), until today, the term *Law of Attraction* is in the minds and on the tongues of millions of people around the world. And yet, because Abraham's words were always changed (probably to avoid infringement of intellectual-property-rights laws), although many millions have now heard some version of the *Law of Attraction,* most have not received sufficient clear information from those abbreviated versions to truly understand this innovative concept well enough to deliberately utilize it. However, many authors *do* credit the Teachings of Abraham for their inspiration, and Esther and I are most appreciative of those creative individuals who do point others back to the source where *they* first learned the depth and power of these principles, as they have been presented to us through Esther by Abraham.

You may find this of interest: In 1965, I discovered Napoleon Hill's classic book *Think and Grow Rich* (and I utilized it deliberately, and it worked for me gloriously!). Hill's principles worked so well for me that, using *Think and Grow Rich* as a textbook, and in conjunction with my business, I began teaching the principles I had been learning to others.

My mission statement was at that time the same as it is today: *It is my intention that the lives of all people I interact with will either be elevated as a result of our interaction, or they will be left where they are, but that no one will be diminished as a result of their association with me.*

After a few years of teaching Hill's principles of success, I came to realize that only a handful of those who were studying with me had achieved the magnitude of success that I was anticipating for *all* of them. And although there were many who did experience significant growth, there were also those who appeared to have no significant financial growth no matter how many success courses they attended.

In the first nine pages of Hill's book, he instructs the readers to look for the *secret*. (He mentions "the hidden secret" 24 times.) Well, I probably read that book over a thousand times between 1965 and 1982, but I was never certain that I ever really knew what "the secret" actually was. I sensed that something was missing. Somehow I sensed that there was another factor in the financial-success equation . . . and so I began to search for the missing link.

During my continued search, even though I read through many books regarding many philosophies, *Think and Grow Rich* was still as close to what I had been asking for as I had been able to find, but much of what Hill knew he didn't include in the book (because it wouldn't have been accepted by the mass market). And much of the *secret* that he *did* put in the book was edited out!

About three years ago, I discovered an unabridged *Think and Grow Rich* manuscript. It had been republished by Melvin Powers's Wilshire Book Company; and as I compared it, word for word, with the version that I had been using for over 40 years, I was amazed to discover that the "secret" had actually been skillfully edited out.

It's no wonder that I was not able to discover Hill's secret: It wasn't there! I won't use the space here to go into much further detail, except to tell you that among many other potent omissions, the word *vibration* was edited out of the book 37 times. (Remember that point—I'll be referring to it later.) And so it turned out that many of the "secrets to success" Napoleon Hill had discovered he didn't even try to publish, and much of the "truth" he *did* try to publish in his first edition was edited out.

And now, let's move forward 70 years to where Esther and I find ourselves amusingly enlightened regarding *our* experience of a publication of a "truth."

A television producer asked Esther and me to allow her to build a television show around our work. She brought her film crew onboard one of our Well-Being Adventure Cruises and filmed the heart of her production around our workshop there on the ship. However, because of a series of fortuitous events, the movie evolved into a DVD format before its Australian network-television airing, and as a result, the project became an enormous success. Millions of people around the world have viewed it. And although the show was named *The Secret* and its advertised intention was to reveal to the world the previously hidden "secret to success," little did the enthusiastic viewers know that the real "secret" that they had been seeking had, once again, been suppressed. . . . In other words, before the show was allowed to be aired, we were informed that The Powers That Be had demanded that, among other things, Abraham's use of the key word *vibration* be edited out of the project.

Esther and I were astonished! Here, seven decades later, the public is again being "protected" from the word *vibration!* And so, it turned out that the real secret behind *The Secret* was that "the secret" was still being kept a secret.

When you're on the inside of an event like this, doesn't it make you wonder how much "truth" *ever* gets past the censors? However, I've come to believe that the reason why most of those innovative philosophical concepts are edited out by the media is not to try to hide the "truth" from the masses, but rather to be able to sell what the marketers believe the people will buy. Also, well-meaning people, in their desire to make innovative ideas more acceptable, often water down or reword new ideas to weaken or buffer the impact of their purity. Abraham has informed us that there is never a crowd on the Leading Edge of thought. However, in this new age of instant Internet connection, we have learned that there are always, among the crowd, Leading Edge thinkers.

Esther and I received the delightful news from our publisher this past week (in March 2007) that our book *The Law of Attraction* (transcribed from our 1985 recordings) has moved up the charts to arrive at the number-two position on the *New York Times* bestseller list. Also, of the millions of books listed on **Amazon.com,** our first Hay House book, *Ask and It Is Given,* has remained among the top 100 books purchased for nearly every day since it came out three years ago. We were told last week that our CD audio book *The Law of Attraction* is at the number-three position of all those available on iTunes; and that beginning this month, the Teachings of Abraham are now on display in Wal-Mart, Sam's Club, Target, and Costco—in other words, they are now available at each of more than 10,000 mass retail outlets and regular bookstores—and the list goes on. (We even had the pleasure and honor, this month, of creating three radio shows with the brilliant—and fun-loving—television host Oprah Winfrey.)

Why am I pointing this out here? Well, now that this information is so readily accessible to mainstream audiences, we're beginning to hear a wide variety of mainstream responses—via various book reviews—and now I've begun reading the online reviews. And, oh, how sweet it is to read of how much pleasure these books are bringing to so many of those who now have the opportunity to learn from them. But *ouch!* The sting of one bee in a bouquet of fragrant flowers! For instance, there are critics who denounce the message because they believe Esther is profiting by "faking" her means of reception of these teachings—in other words, "she says she's channeling" so that readers will buy the books. And then there are those opposite critics who would denounce the information because they *do* believe that Esther is receiving these teachings directly from Abraham, but they have been told by the programmers of *their* conscience that there is something wrong with allowing a book to be written in that manner. . . . How would you please them all?

Well, we learned long ago that no one can please everyone, so we decided early in 1985 to self-publish our material so that we could make available whatever practical information we would receive from Abraham (uncensored) in its purity to those who are asking the questions that are being answered by Abraham.

When Louise Hay requested that we ask Abraham to write a comprehensive book and allow Hay House to publish it (*Ask and It Is Given*, 2004), she stated to her executives: "We will inform our entire staff that Abraham's words are not to be changed during the editing process. We are going to *allow* Abraham's teachings to reach out, in their purity, into the entire world."

Esther and I are indescribably pleased that Louise and her publishing company are in the process of fulfilling that intention of providing this magnificent material, in its pure form, to those people of the world who are asking for it—and we also appreciate those people of the world who are asking for it. We do adore facilitating the publication of yet another magnificent book that will continue the dissemination of the Teachings of Abraham, but our greatest joy is in the translation—the creation—of the information.

There is nothing that pleases Esther or me more than providing a forum where people from diverse environments can gather, lending their unique perspectives, asking Abraham their important questions. To actually feel the evolution and expansion of this message—as it is honed and finely tuned by the never-ending questions of those like you—must surely be what Esther and I have been born to do. And the reason we know that is because *it feels so very, very good to do it.*

— From my heart, Jerry Hicks

∾∾∾ ∾∾∾

(**Editor's Note:** Please note that since there aren't always physical English words to perfectly express the Non-Physical thoughts that Esther receives, she sometimes forms new combinations of words, as well as using standard words in new ways—for example, capitalizing them when normally they wouldn't be—in order to express new ways of looking at old ways of looking at life.)

Esther and Abraham Are Ready to Begin

Esther: Hi, Abraham. I know you already know this, but I just wanted to begin by telling you that I am really enjoying translating your information at this time. Writing the books and doing the seminars is such a wonderful experience for me. I love the feeling of you, pouring through me.

It is my intention to sit every morning for a few hours and allow you to write this new book. I think I may have found the perfect environment in which to do this. I personally have never been in a more beautiful or better-feeling space. I feel really good about everything, and I attribute my tremendous improvement in the way I feel to your recent discussions about the Stream—the *upstream/downstream* analogies.

Anyway, I just wanted to chat with you a little before we begin here to tell you that I love you, that I love working with you, and that I want to do this forever.

I'll close my eyes and breathe, and I will write your words as I receive them.

Abraham: Esther, this is an interesting process. Do you agree? We have an entire book (actually, endless books) ready for you to receive. The *asking* has taken place, by your world and by you and Jerry, and the book has been *given* and stands in Vibrational Escrow, ready for you. And so, now it really is up to you to find the time and the alignment to receive it.

We know that you have always sensed this because you have had the experience on so many occasions of preparing yourself in readiness to receive our words, but now, in light of so many recent discussions, you are even more aware of the value of the part that you play. Everything that everyone wants has been given. But to receive it, to see it, to have it, you must—under all conditions—become a Vibrational Match with it.

It is a delicate blend of releasing your awareness of your physical world enough to align with the vibration that is Abraham, while at the same time maintaining enough of your connection with your physical world to receive us and translate our message into something that is meaningful and understandable by your world. This balance requires the remarkable stability and clarity that you have achieved.

And so, let us begin the writing of another wonderful book.

PART I

Discovering the Astonishing Power of Emotions

Chapter One

Abraham Welcomes Us
All to Planet Earth

So here you are, living your life in your wonderful body on this magnificent planet, and while it is not the first day of your arrival here, we would like to welcome you to planet Earth.

Since you have been here for a while, it may seem strange that we are now welcoming you, but we do so because we want to help you gain a new viewpoint of this lifetime, of your existence, and of *you!*

We have a clear view of you in your current life experience, but we also have the ability to step back and see you and your life in a much broader context than you can see it from your current perspective. It is our desire that our explanation of you, in its broader view, will assist you in realizing the perfection in this Eternal plan of life.

We know that your birth into your physical body seems as if it was the beginning of that which you are, but it was far from the beginning of you. It is a bit like your walking into a movie theater and feeling that your entry into this theater is the beginning of you.

You might argue, from your physical point of view, that walking into a movie theater is far different from being born into your body as an infant, because when you enter the theater, you do not forget what happened before you entered. You remember who you were and what you were doing before you walked into the theater. You have a keen sense of continuity about "before" you walked into the theater as it relates to "being in" the theater and what "comes after" being in the theater. In other words, it does not feel to you as if a new life began for you when you entered the theater.

But we are attempting to stretch your perception a little so that you can begin to realize that when you were born into the body, which you now refer to as "you," you were not "beginning" then, either. It is our desire to reawaken within you that broader sense of continuity as you start to remember who you were "before" you came into this body; and even more, it is our desire that you allow yourself to *become* that Broader Perspective, focused here and now, but remembering *who-you-really-are* and why you have come forth into this body.

Also, you might say, "But unlike the day I was born, when I walked into the movie theater I was mature—I was able to speak and walk and feed myself." And while we certainly understand why your small size and physical immaturity makes it seem as if you were only then beginning, that is not the case. *Your new body and new surroundings provide a new opportunity for a very wise and very old Being to continue to expand in new ways.*

As your Broader Perspective of *who-you-really-are* awakens within you, your appreciation of this life experience will be tremendously enhanced. As you look at life on planet Earth in this greater context, your fears will be diminished and your natural eagerness for life will explode within you.

The Value of Your Faith

So here we stand, looking at you and your life in its broadest of contexts, attempting to explain it to you from where you now stand. But you cannot see "you" from our perspective . . . and, of course, when you do see yourself from our perspective, then our explanation will be unnecessary anyway.

In this section of the book, we are going to express our perspective of you, and of us, and how we relate to one another. We cannot impress our viewpoint upon you. However, as you read these words and ponder them fully in an attitude of faith or wanting to understand, together we will build enough bridges as you move through the pages of this book so that as you turn the last page of the book, you will be able to understand and hold our viewpoint— not because our words will have been so powerful that they will have transformed you, but because the combination of the logic of our words and the unfolding of your own life will transform your *faith* or *hope* into *knowing.*

And what a wonderful state of Being . . . to *know,* with absolute certainty, the existence of your Being and the reason for your existence, and to have a full realization of *all-that-you-are.* And then, you can get on with what you came to do: *live your eternally expanding life in joy!*

This Glorious Planet Thrilled You

While the idea of coming forth into a new physical body on planet Earth was certainly not a new idea to you, it was an absolutely exhilarating idea, for from your Non-Physical perspective, prior to your physical birth, you understood all of the implications of this new birth. You understood the perfect and stable environment into which you would be born, and you felt unbounded enthusiasm for its variety.

What you felt most was the freedom and unlimited nature of this environment. The diverse beauty of the physical nature of your planet thrilled you as you anticipated your arrival, but you were also thrilled with the beauty of the diversity of the people and ideas that were waiting for you. At no point in your preparation for making your new entrance into this physical body did you feel concern about the perspective of the inhabitants of your planet. Not once did you feel a need to get here so that you could set them straight, or show them the error of their ways, or correct their course.

You saw this planet as diverse, ever changing, and perfect; and you came forth with an eagerness that defies verbal description. And because of the secure vantage point from which you were coming, you were not guarded or concerned about your entrance or about what would surround you once you got here. Instead, you knew that you had within you the resources not only to cope with your new environment, but also to mine it for the joyous expansion that you are eternally about. And so here you are—and while you did not just get here, everything that you have just read still holds true.

It is our desire to restore your understanding to what it was just before you came forth into this body so that you can *now* experience this magnificent life experience in this wonderful body, on this glorious planet, in the way that you intended.

So, dear friends, welcome to planet Earth.

ఆ ఆ ఆ ఏ ఏ ఏ

Chapter Two

Remembering the Big Picture

While we are eager to get to the heart of this book—which is a complete explanation of the power and value of your emotions and how to understand them and effectively utilize the guidance that they provide—it is necessary that we first give you a broader view of your Eternal nature.

While this description of you may seem foreign to you upon your first reading, as you absorb it and consider it fully, you will begin to feel a recognition of this view, for at deeper and broader levels of your own Being, you already know this. And so, these words will help you remember: *By your physical standards, where you define your experience in physical terms with physical places and such, you would likely define the Non-Physical realm as a Non-Place. But even though Non-Physical differs from physical in many ways, and while you cannot perceive it accurately from your physical perspective, it exists, it is real, it is vast—and it is a place (or rather, a Non-Place) of Pure, Positive Energy.*

Prior to your emergence into this physical body, you were fully aware and conscious in the Non-Physical realm. In other words, you understood yourself as *you* in the same way that you now identify yourself as *you*. And in the same way that you stand in your physical body, looking out into your world, translating what you see through the lens of your own personal perspective, from your Non-Physical vantage point, you also translate everything that you behold from your own powerful, personal perspective. The Non-Physical You has an eternally expanding identity through which you perceive life; and from that vantage point, you *observe,* you *think,* you *imagine,* you *ponder,* you *know,* and you *feel.*

So, from that broad Non-Physical perspective, you came forth into this physical body. *You came as an extension of the Pure, Positive Energy Being that you are in the Non-Physical. And as you were born and you donned the body and personality that you and others identify as you, that conscious Being that existed in the Non-Physical realm still exists there. In the same way that a thinker thinks a thought but still exists separately from the thought he or she thinks, the Non-Physical You* thought *you but still exists separately from the* you *that was thought. In other words, when you give birth to an idea, you still exist to give birth to another idea.*

And so, from your Non-Physical vantage point, you gave birth to the physical you. And when the vibrational projection of thought, which extended from the Non-Physical into the physical, converged with the physical body that was conceived and grew in your mother's womb, you were born. So what was once an *idea,* which was considered and imagined, has now become a physical reality. The *idea* of you has now become a physical reality; and the Non-Physical You who gave birth to the idea remains Non-Physically focused, and so because of your physical birth, it has now become even more fully expanded.

So now not only has the Non-Physical You expanded, but you now have two powerful points of view: your physical viewpoint and your Non-Physical viewpoint. And there is nothing that will ever be more important for either of these two wonderful perspectives than their relationship to each other. Everything that you are living is about your physical and Non-Physical points of view and how they interplay with one another.

The reason we are writing this book is to help you understand that through discovering the astonishing power of your emotions, then and only then can you clearly understand your relationship with the Non-Physical You.

Your Relationship with Your Inner Being

Now, as we define and describe these two important aspects of you, rather than referring to them as *you* and *You,* it will be more clarifying to refer to the physical you as *you* and the Non-Physical aspect of you as your *Inner Being.* You could call your *Inner Being Source, Soul,* or *God,* but we like the name *Inner Being,* since it is the root of that which you are, and you can feel it within you.

So from your Non-Physical perspective, your *Inner Being* projected its Consciousness into the physical you. And you were born. And now here you are, living, breathing, thinking, and being—and at the same time, your *Inner Being* is living, thinking, and being.

We like to refer to this time and place in which you are focused as the Leading Edge of thought, and when you think about your broader, Non-Physical *Inner Being* extending itself forward into this life experience, it is easier to understand that this physical realm in which you are focused surely is the furthermost extension of that which is Source.

Humans hold a variety of beliefs regarding their pre-physical origin, but a very common thread weaves through many of those beliefs—which is actually exactly the opposite of the way it really is—and that incorrect belief is that God is Non-Physical, and therefore perfect, and therefore complete in that perfection; and that a human has been given physical life in order to work to achieve that perfection, or to catch up with God.

What we want you to remember is that you, in your physical body, are an extension of that which humans call *God.* And because you are the furthermost extension of God (or *Source*), then God is also experiencing that expansion because of you, through you, and with you.

When we use the word *God* to express this Non-Physical Source Energy, we find that because it reminds people of the ideas they already hold around this word, it often prevents them from being able to find the deeper clarity that we seek to provide—and for that reason, we rarely describe this Non-Physical Source Energy with the word *God.* The word *God* just activates within most of you what you already think about the subject, so instead of the label *God,* we will use the label *Source* . . . and this *Non-Physical Source* experiences constant expansion through you, even when you are unaware of its existence or of its connection to you.

৵৵৵ ৶৶৶

Chapter Three

The Universe Continues to Expand Through You

So, you were Non-Physical Source Energy (and still are), and from that Non-Physical vantage point, you projected a part of your Consciousness here into this physical body. And so, here you are, exploring the wonderful detail and contrast of this Leading-Edge time-space reality.

Now, here in your physical body, you are surrounded by wonderful specific details of contrasting life experience that you are able to decipher through your physical senses. And as you live your life—day by day and segment by segment—your personal deciphering of life causes a further expansion of the Universe.

As you observe your world, you are seeing it through *your* eyes; hearing it through *your* ears; and smelling it, tasting it, touching it through *your* deciphering senses. In other words, you cannot help but see your world through your personal and important perspective of self. And in that natural process of perceiving life from your perspective of self, you cannot help but give birth to new preferences and to desires for things that from your perspective would be even better still. In other words, by living life from your selfish point of view, you are discovering improvements.

Many of our physical friends do not like the idea of being selfish, but that is because they misunderstand a fundamental principle of life: *You cannot be other than selfish, for you cannot observe, perceive, or be other than from your perspective of self. All points of Consciousness, even one-celled organisms, perceive. And they do so from the ever-changing selfish perspective that they currently hold.*

Even Without Words, You Are Creating

As you live your life, having personal experiences and observing experiences that others are living, you often see things that you clearly *do not* want. And each time that occurs, a clarification of what you *do* want erupts within you. Occasionally the experience is so dramatic that you could clearly state, "I don't want that! And I now understand that what I want instead is . . ."

You always know more clearly what you do want when you are faced with what you do not want. But whether you are consciously aware of it or not, all day, every day, you are giving birth to new desires that are being born from the details of the life you are living out on the Leading Edge of thought.

Most humans are not aware of this process of expansion. Even when they read these words explaining it, most do not find it of any particular significance to their own life experience. But from your Non-Physical perspective, before you came forth into this body, you found it compelling. In fact, there was no thought that was more exhilarating to you, because you understood then that the entire expansion of the Universe occurs in just that way. You knew that your Leading Edge experience on planet Earth would literally inspire expansion within you, and that the delicious contrast of this time-space reality was the stuff that puts the Eternalness in Eternity. But, of course, from that Non-Physical perspective, you were able to see the entire picture of creation and expansion—and that is why we are reminding you again of it now.

Your *Inner Being* Flows with New Desires

And so, whether you are consciously aware of your new expanded desire or not, desire is born out of the contrast you are living . . . for during that process of you knowing what you do not want, the clear, expanded idea of what you prefer instead is born, and your *Inner Being* (or the *Source* within you) turns its undivided attention to that new expanded idea!

Now this is the most important part of this story of creation and of your physical, human, Leading Edge creative part in it: *In the moment that a new-and-improved version of life is born out of the life you are living, you have the option of aligning with the new idea or of resisting it.* And the choice that you make in that moment is really what this book is all about—but, even more important, it is what your life of joy (or of misery) is about, for that is the point of your joyfully allowing you to be *You* (or not).

So, from your Non-Physical perspective (or *Source* perspective) before your birth into this physical body, you eagerly understood these things:

- You would be focused in a physical body.

- You would be living amongst a wide variety of contrast.

- The contrast that you would be living would stimulate new ideas of improvement and expansion within you.

- The broader, Non-Physical part of you (your *Inner Being*) would embrace the new ideas fully and would literally become their vibrational equivalent.

Thought Always Precedes Manifestation

In the creation of everything that exists, thought always comes first. Everything that you see around you was once a thought or an idea—a vibrational concept that matured into what you call physical reality.

When standing on the furthermost expanded edge of any creation, it is not possible to see back far enough to comprehend its beginning, but everything that exists in what you see as reality or manifested form was at one time an idea that was thought upon long enough that, by the *Law of Attraction,* it reached the maturity in which you now behold it. Nothing exists that is outside of this process of creation.

Your planet was conceived from the Non-Physical realm long before that which you call human walked upon it, and as that

Non-Physical focus, from what humans call *Source,* was cast upon the idea of it, your wondrous Leading Edge time-space reality was created. . . . *First, there is thought, and as more thought is offered to any subject, the thought begins to take form until there is manifestation of that which humans call "reality." So not unlike the creation of the planet itself, as you stand in your physical bodies—as manifested extensions of that which you call Source—you continue the creation of your planet, and life upon it, through your thought.*

As you know what you *do not* want, you know more clearly what you *do* want, and so an improved idea is born from the contrast you are living. As you sift through the details of your life experience, day by day and moment by moment, you radiate a constant barrage of vibrational offerings (we call them *rockets of desire*) outward. *With each vibrational rocket of desire, the Source within you—the Source from which you have come, the Source still focused from the Non-Physical perspective—focuses intently upon your newly expanded version of life, and becomes it. And as this never-ending process continues from you living life and coming to new-and-improved conclusions about what you desire (at both spoken and unspoken levels), that broader Non-Physical part of you expands.*

Your hopes and dreams and intentions and ideas for improvement are held for you in a sort of *Vibrational Escrow;* and that escrow account, if you will, is held for you, tended for you, and nurtured for you, waiting for your withdrawal from it. Not only is it being held for you, but the larger part of you has already become it and is constantly and eternally calling the physical part of you toward it. So now, what is actually happening is that the physical you is being called forward by the Non-Physical You for the completion of the idea that you have given birth to; and in its purest, nonresisted form, that calling feels to you like passion or enthusiasm.

And so, now, the most important question is: *Are you letting you join the newly created, newly expanded version of You?* And the answer to that all-important question lies in the way that you *feel.* The better you feel, the more you are allowing that Connection; and the worse you feel, the more you are disallowing, or resisting, that Connection.

When you feel love or joy—or any positive emotion—you are literally being the expanded version that life has caused you to become. When you feel fear, anger, or despair—or any negative emotion—you are not, in this moment, by virtue of whatever it is that you are giving your attention to, allowing yourself to be that new expanded version . . . you are not letting yourself keep up with who you have become.

≈≈≈ ≈≈≈

Chapter Four

You Are a Vibrational Being

You perceive your current physical environment through the utilization of your physical senses. This interpretation of your environment happens so naturally—without the necessity of deliberate attention or focus—that most of our physical friends have no conscious realization that they are interpreting vibration into what they see, hear, smell, taste, and touch.

As you watch your television, you understand that the people and places you are seeing are not miniature versions of life playing out inside the small box or the thin screen that you are watching. You understand that the machine is somehow receiving signals and translating them into meaningful images and displaying them on the monitor for your viewing pleasure. And while analogies are never perfect, the idea we want you to consider is that in a similar manner, *you are the receiver of vibrational signals that you are translating through your physical senses into the reality that you are living. And as you interact with so many other Vibrational Beings, together you are creating an extraordinary reality.*

You did not need training from other wise physical friends in order to utilize your eyes in order to see. Hearing, smelling, tasting, and the sensation of touch through your skin also came so naturally to you that no discussion on *how* to do it was necessary. In other words, you were born into a physical body that contained within its cells the knowledge of translating vibration into meaningful life experience.

You Have a Sixth Sense

Beyond the five physical senses that you are actively aware of, there is another less-realized sense—the sense of emotion.

Just as with your other five senses, that sixth sense, which was active within you on the day you were born, requires no training in order for you to understand that it exists. Just as no one taught you to see or to hear, smell, taste, or touch, you do not need training in order to recognize that you are *feeling* emotions. In fact, your awareness of your emotions is evidenced by the conversations you have as you define your life experience and your awareness of it. You often explain how you "feel" about this or that: "My feelings are hurt," "I feel happy," "I feel bad," "I feel lonely," or "I feel guilty."

Emotions play a large role in the life experience of you and everyone you know, but few have any conscious awareness of the astonishing power and value of their emotions. It is our intention here to assist you, in the reading of these words, to come to a fuller conscious understanding of your emotions: how it is that they exist; what they mean; and most important, how to utilize your awareness of them in a meaningful way. We intend to explain to you that your emotions are literally your indication of how *you* are blending with *You.*

So Back to the Big Picture

You were Non-Physically focused—and still are. You projected a part of that Non-Physical Consciousness into your current physical body, and so you are born into this body. Utilizing your physical senses, you perceive your environment and give birth to continuing new rockets of desire. The Non-Physical part of you that still remains Non-Physically focused sees your new desire and gives full attention to it and literally becomes it—and now stands as the vibrational equivalent of this new, expanded version of you.

All day, every day, your physical life experience causes you to expand. With each encounter with other people, with the things you read, with the things you see, with experiences you have, you give birth to continual rockets of desire. When someone is rude to you, you desire that others are kinder. When you are misunderstood, you desire to be understood. When you do not have enough money, wellness, or friendship, you want more of those things. *Life causes you to constantly become more.* In other words, a new-and-improved you (by your standards and perceptions) is in a constant state of becoming, for the Non-Physical part of you is constantly becoming whatever it is that you are asking for.

Chapter Five

Your Emotions Are Absolute Indicators

So when your perception of your current life experience causes a realization that you do not have enough of something—such as money, time, clarity, or stamina—your desire evolves. Whenever you know what is lacking, you know more clearly what it is that you desire. In other words, in the midst of sickness, your desire for wellness is always clearly amplified. And as your desires evolve all day, every day, that Non-Physical part of you evolves, because that part of you also flows with the new ideas and desires in the moment that you give birth to each and every one of them.

If you were as sure of *who-you-are* as the inner part of you is, you also could turn your undivided attention toward the new ideas; and if you were to do that, you would feel an eagerness for life, a clarity of mind, and a vitality of body that would be indescribably wonderful. In other words, if you were able to keep up with You, the exhilaration of that Connection would be delicious. And conversely, when you do not allow yourself to keep up with who you have become, you feel the discomfort of that resistance.

The emotions that you feel, in any moment of life, are the indicators of the vibrational relationship between you and You; your emotions are telling you whether your current active thought and subsequent vibrational offering matches the vibration of your evolved *Source* self or not. When the signals match—or come close to matching—you feel wonderful. When the signals do not match, you do not feel so good. And so, an awareness of your emotions and what they mean is essential to your conscious evolution. In very plain and simple terms, *you must find a way to allow yourself to keep up with what life is causing you to become if you are to live the joyous life you came here to live.*

Your Expansion Is Constant

If your observation of your life experience causes you to realize that you do not have enough money to do some of the things you want to do, your desire for more money is amplified, and your Vibrational Escrow now expands to include that desire. Everything that happens throughout your day that causes you to realize that you want or need more money causes additional amendments to your desire regarding your financial abundance.

If your observation of your life experience causes you to realize that your body does not look or feel the way you want it to, your desire for that improved bodily condition is amplified, and your Vibrational Escrow now expands to include that desire, also.

If your interaction with other people at your place of work causes you to realize that you are not appreciated, your desire for appreciation is amplified. When you are bored with what you are doing, your desire for more stimulating things to work on is amplified. When someone at work is promoted and given a raise, your desire for more recognition or appreciation is then amplified. *When you do not have a significant relationship, your desire for one is amplified. When your current relationship feels like a struggle, your desire for a more compatible relationship is amplified.*

In every waking moment of your life, you are utilizing the data that makes up the details of your life in order to expand—and this expansion is constant. And with every detail that you chew upon, you exude vibrational requests for improvement, and the broader part of you (your *Inner Being,* or *Source*) becomes that expanded version that your life has asked for.

It Is All about Aligning Your Thoughts

So you have now read several times in the beginning pages of this book our words that *you must allow yourself to keep up with that which you are becoming if you are to live the joyful life that you have come forth to live.* This important premise is not only the basis of this valuable book, but it is the foundation of your joyful life experience.

We do not see many of you taking issue with the idea that when you do not have enough of something that you want, your desire to *have* it is even more amplified. And no one questions that once you have identified that you really *want* something, you would feel better in the *having* of it. But there is a very important distinction that we want you to understand that will help you mold your life into that which pleases you: *This is a __mental__ process, not an __action__ process. It is about aligning your thoughts; it is not about taking action in order to achieve results.*

When your life causes you to realize that you want more money, we are not suggesting that you get another job or change your activities in some way to get more money.

When your life causes you to realize that you have 50 pounds more body weight than you desire, we are not suggesting that you go on a strict diet or begin intense exercise to reduce your weight.

When you are unappreciated at work, we are not suggesting that you confront someone, demanding more appreciation, or that you quit your job and try to find another position where appreciation is offered more easily.

Allowing yourself to become what life has caused you to desire is not about action. It is about the aligning of thought Energies. It is about focusing your attention in the direction of your desire rather than looking back at the current conditions that have given birth to your desire. And while you may very well eventually become inspired to some action, it is the alignment of thought Energy (a vibrational alignment) that you are seeking.

When you achieve vibrational alignment, any inspired action will feel wonderful.

Without the vibrational alignment, any action taken will feel difficult.

With the vibrational alignment, your every effort will yield wonderful results or return on your time.

Without the vibrational alignment, the outcome of your effort will be disappointing, resulting in discouragement as you conclude, "This just doesn't work for me."

ᐂᐂᐂ ᐂᐂᐂ

Chapter Six

Vibrational Alignment Feels Like Relief

When we speak of vibrational alignment, we are referring to aligning the vibrations within *your Being only.* It has nothing to do with anything that anyone else is doing. This sometimes raises a question in those who hear us say that, because it seems to many people that the only problems they have are due to their interaction with other people: "So doesn't something need to be done about *those* individuals?"

It is true, you are interacting with others, and often that interaction is the source of your discomfort or problem, but asking *them* to be different is not the answer. Most of them are not willing to change for you anyway, and even when they *are* willing, they cannot consistently be what you need them to be in order for you to feel good. The answer to your feeling good is only in the alignment of the Energy within you. As we have said before, it is about you allowing yourself to keep up with what the larger part of you has become.

For example, let us say that you are having a perfectly nice day: You have rested well, you have eaten well, and you are happily involved in a project that is pleasing to you—and then someone you care about comes to you with a problem. Not only is there a problem, but the person also thinks that you should take some sort of action to solve the problem. This could be your mate, one of your children, an employee, a client, a friend, or perhaps even someone you do not know. In this example, let us say that one of your employees whom you love and care about is having an interpersonal-relationship problem with other employees, whom you also care deeply about.

As you listen to this person presenting his or her perspective on the situation, you begin to feel your happiness diminishing, your vitality diminishing, your clarity diminishing; and now you feel sad, tired, and confused. You listen politely, and your mind races to find solutions. . . . You find yourself relating to what this person is telling you as you hear his or her description of the situation. And you begin to feel overwhelmed as you realize that you really do not have enough knowledge or time to gather enough information to make a rational decision about how to solve this problem. You want to gather the information, perhaps talk with others involved, in order to get a clear view of the situation, but as you take the action of more discussion and begin to make suggestions for changes in policies or activities, you feel worse still.

The more you listen and discuss—and the more people you talk with about the situation—the more powerless you feel as you realize that you cannot begin to unravel this situation and get to the bottom of it. And while you have the power to make sweeping decisions (in fact, if they were employees, you could fire them all and begin again with a fresh and willing new group), you can feel the futility of that action as well.

While you usually are not aware of it at the time, a wonderful opportunity for expansion is occurring, because in the midst of this uncomfortable turmoil, you are giving birth to expanded rockets of desire. With every part of this situation in which you know what you do not want, a counter rocket of desire is launched, and the broader Non-Physical part of you has become a *Vibrational Match* to that expanded desire. And the discomfort that you are feeling right now—which seems like a response to what your employee is complaining about—is actually the discord between your current thought of what has gone wrong and the expanded desire that your *Inner Being* is newly embracing.

The vibrations within you are now out of alignment, and when you are out of vibrational alignment, there is no *action* that will solve the problem. You will not find effective actions or words, or even thoughts or ideas, from your place of misalignment. In fact, any of that which is attempted from your place of misalignment will only serve to make matters worse.

If we were standing in your physical shoes, our every effort would be pointed toward one result: We would be looking for a way, any way, to feel better. We would do our best, from where we stand, to find a way of finding some sort of emotional relief about this unsettled subject, because when some relief is discovered, you are on the way to an alignment of Energy.

Putting Your Canoe into the Stream

Imagine putting your canoe, with oars already inside, in a river and floating on the current, and then deliberately turning your canoe upstream and paddling with all of your strength *against* the flow. And as we see you in your boat, paddling very hard against the current, we ask, "What do you think about turning your canoe *downstream* and going *with* the current?"

And most reply, "Turn downstream? Oh, that just seems lazy!"

"But how long can you keep that up?" we ask.

"I'm not sure," most answer, "but it is my duty or responsibility to figure that out."

And then, if we were to visit long with most people, they would go on to explain: "This is just what we all do here." "It's what my mother did, and her mother before her." "Anyone who amounts to anything works diligently *against* the current." "All trophies and monuments are erected to honor those hardworking people who stayed strong *against* the current."

"And anyway," people often remind us, "there are even more rewards after we die for those who work hard like this."

We watch you getting more efficient at fighting the current. Your muscles get stronger, your boats become sleeker, and you discover more effective oars. And, always, we listen patiently as we hear a variety of versions on this same general theme of justification for paddling *upstream,* but then we always explain what we consider to be the most important thing that our physical friends could ever hear from us: *Nothing that you want is <u>upstream</u>!*

The reason we are so certain that nothing that you want is *upstream* is because we understand the Stream. We have seen it in its origin, and we watch it as it increases in size and speed. We know what the Current is and why it flows the way it does, and we understand where this Stream will lead you if you will but allow it.

This is the Stream of Life, and it was in motion before you came forth into your physical body. And, from your Non-Physical perspective, as you set forth your intentions to be here on this planet in this body, you added to the Current of this fast-moving Stream. And now, focused in this physical body, you continue to add to the Current of the Stream by sifting through the data of your life and coming to personal conclusions about what you *do not* want, which produces the natural asking for what you *do* want. For, with every asking, whether of great or small importance, you add to the speed of the Current of the Stream.

Whenever your life causes you to ask for something beyond what you are living, the Non-Physical part of you rides that rocket of desire and literally becomes the vibrational fulfillment of your request. . . . Every question you ask causes a formulation of an answer, and your *Inner Being* focuses upon that answer. Every problem you face causes a formulation of a solution; and your *Inner Being* not only focuses upon that solution, but also literally becomes it vibrationally.

If you will allow it, this Stream, this fast-moving Current, will carry you <u>downstream</u> to the fulfillment of everything that your life has caused you to create—for it is all there for you, in a sort of Vibrational Escrow, waiting for you to flow to it.

Your <u>Inner Being</u> Has Already Become It

When your life causes you to ask for something beyond where you are, the *broader Non-Physical, Source Energy, Inner Being* part of you becomes the *vibrational equivalent* of what you are asking for. We talked about that earlier when we explained that you are continually evolving, and that with everything that life causes you to ask for, your *Inner Being* becomes that expanded you.

The *Law of Attraction* is the most powerful *Law* in the Universe—it is the vibrational manager of all that exists. Everything that exists—seen or unseen, tangible or invisible, electronic or materialistic, physical or Non-Physical—is not only affected, but is managed, by this powerful *Universal Law*. In simple terms, this *Law* says: *The essence of that which is like unto itself, is drawn.* Whether they are contemplating the well-documented physics of electronics or noticing that their own habitual thoughts are rendering them circumstances and experiences that perfectly match their moods and attitudes regarding all things, many are consciously recognizing the basis of this powerful *Law* in their own experiences.

The powerful *Law of Attraction* is responding to the vibration of that which the greater part of you has become, and as the *Law of Attraction* responds to the vibration of the expanded you, the Current flows, for the Current of this Stream of Life is literally the momentum that is caused by the *Law of Attraction's* response to the vibration of your expanded Being.

The big question—the question that this book seeks to answer—is: What are you, in your physical form, doing in relationship to the vibration of your expanded self? Are you letting yourself be up to vibrational speed with what you have become or not?

Chapter Seven

The Vibrational Gap
Between You and *You*

Because life has caused you to expand, and because the *Law of Attraction* is now responding to the vibration of that expanded you, you can now consciously feel your response to that moving Energy.

That is precisely what your emotions are. If the thoughts you are thinking, in this moment, are in alignment with the vibration of the Broader You, you feel the harmony of that alignment in the form of positive-feeling emotions. But if the thoughts you are thinking in this moment are out of alignment with the vibration of the Broader You, you feel the *dis*harmony of that alignment in the form of negative emotions.

So, going back to the analogy of you in your canoe in the Stream: *When you are allowing yourself to float freely in the Stream, without resistance, thus closing the gap between where you are right now and who the broader part of you has become, you feel your alignment in the form of positive emotion. But if you are still paddling <u>upstream,</u> holding yourself against the natural Current of your own evolution, your resistance to the Stream and to that which the larger part of you has become is evidenced in the form of negative emotion.*

The Power of Your Guiding Emotions

If someone you did not know contacted you in some way and said to you, "Hello, you don't know me, but I wanted to tell you that I'll never contact you in any way again," you would say, "All right." You would not feel sad or disappointed that you would not hear from this stranger again. But if someone important to you were to tell you that, you would feel strong negative emotion.

The emotion that you feel always indicates the vibrational difference between your point of desire and your current thought. You could say that your emotions indicate the difference between your desire and your belief, or between your desire and your expectation. We like to explain that your emotions indicate the vibrational relationship between the vibration of who you have really become and who you are allowing yourself to be right now because of the thoughts you are thinking.

For example, when you are feeling proud of yourself, the feelings that you are experiencing are indicating alignment between the vibration (or thought) of your *Inner Being* and the vibration (or thought) of you right here, right now. When you feel ashamed or embarrassed, those feelings indicate that you, in your now, are thinking thoughts about yourself that are very different from the thoughts that the Broader part of you is having about you.

Before your emotions can be meaningful to you—before you can allow them to give you the precise and perfect guidance that they are offering—you must understand that you are a Being with two points of perspective that are continually relating to each other. When you understand that your *Inner Being,* or the *expanded Being* that you are becoming, stands as the furthermost culmination of life and constantly calls you forward to that, then you begin to understand the feeling of passion or eagerness that is present when you are allowing your movement toward your expanded self. And you also understand the feeling of being unfulfilled or of uneasiness when you are not allowing your movement toward your expanded self.

There is just no way of getting around it: You must allow yourself to be the Being that life is causing you to become if you are to feel joy. And unless you are feeling joy, you are not allowing yourself to be that which life has caused you to become.

Emotions Indicate the Degree of Your Alignment

As you know from your own life experience, a variety of feelings move through you depending upon what is happening, what you are observing, and what you are thinking. Your emotion, whether it feels good or bad, is a vibrational indicator of the relationship between the vibration of your Broader Self and you. Your emotions indicate the degree of your alignment with who you have become. They show you if, in this moment, you are keeping up with yourself or not.

Over time, you have come to describe the variety of feelings or emotions with many different words. And because of the number of individuals who have felt these emotions, and because of the many generations of people having a variety of experiences, you have come to a somewhat consistent agreement on what you are feeling and the word you would use to describe it.

We would much prefer that you find yourself in feelings of <u>eagerness</u> and <u>love</u> and <u>joy</u> than in those of <u>fear</u> or <u>hatred</u> or <u>anger,</u> but because we understand the vibrational reason for these emotions, we do not attempt to guide you from the emotion of <u>fear</u> directly to the emotion of <u>joy,</u> for we understand that the vibrational difference is too great to span all at once. And, in fact, we see no reason to try to make the jump all at once, because a gradual movement in the direction of feeling better is all that is necessary or even possible.

Nothing That You Want Is <u>Upstream</u>

Everything that you see around you (land, sky, rivers, buildings, and even people and animals) was *thought-vibration* before it became the physical things you now observe. While most do not realize it, you are standing on the Leading Edge of thought. Further, you are so good at translating vibration through your senses of sight, hearing, smell, taste, and touch that for the most part you are unaware of the translation process at all. It is just life, and you are living it.

But if you can grasp the concept that everything that you see around you in manifested form was *thought-vibration* first, and then *thought-form,* and finally the *manifestation* as you see it now, the bigger picture of creation will begin to come into view for you. And then not only will you have a clearer picture of how things that you call "real life experience" come to be, but you will also *feel* the Current from which all things come and upon which all things flow.

What we mean when we say "Nothing that you want is *upstream*" is that your desires—because you have already thought about them and asked for them—are already in the process of being created. *In the same way that a round object will roll downhill of its own accord without needing an engine or added impetus from outside influences, your desires are, in a sense, easily and naturally rolling toward their own conclusions as well. Once your life has caused the creation of a desire, your work is done, and natural forces and laws will take over.*

The best way we have come to explain to you this pattern of natural evolution is in our analogy of the Current of the river: *Your every request, large or small, adds to the Current of this river; and literally everything that you have ever asked for is <u>downstream,</u> where you can easily find it, experience it, possess it, or live it.*

ᵒᵍᵒᵍᵒᵍ ᶜᵉᶜᵉᶜᵉ

Chapter Eight

Your Life Flows in a Natural Cycle

We like the analogy of you in your canoe on the river because it points out the futility of trying to paddle against the Current. When you remember that you are *Source Energy*, that you came into this body from *Source*, and that now in this body, you are giving birth to Leading Edge desires—which *Source* then becomes and calls you toward—you understand the real River of Life. And then you understand the futility of trying to paddle *upstream* against this Current.

If you will consider these important ideas and integrate them into your thinking until they become the cornerstone of that which you are, you will then be able to get on with what you intended when you came forth into this body. You will then be able to live the joyous life experience that you came forth to live.

- Before your birth, from your perspective of *Source*, you set forth the thought of coming forth into this physical body.

- From your *Source* perspective, you gave birth to the idea or thought of *you*.

- The *Law of Attraction* responded to that idea and called forth the manifestation of *you*.

- Now in this body, you give birth to expanded ideas of your life.

- The *Law of Attraction* now responds to those ideas and calls them forth into manifestation.

- Now, from an existing perspective, another thought is given.

- The *Law of Attraction* responds to that thought, and momentum is created.

- And that momentum—caused by the *Law of Attraction*'s response to thought—is the Current of Life.

As you consciously accept the Eternal nature of your Being, the idea of never-ending expansion is an easy concept to follow.

As you consciously accept that you are an eternally expanding Being, then living life in this fantastically diverse physical environment, where new ideas are continually born, makes perfect sense.

As you understand that you are that Eternal Being at the same time that you are physically focused here, you begin to see the process of creation in an even clearer way.

When you remember that the *Inner Being* part of you always responds to the expanded idea that your physical life has given birth to, you begin to get a sense of the momentum of this Stream.

And, finally, when you understand that the *Law of Attraction* is responding to that furthermost idea with the same Energy that creates worlds, you then get a further sense of the momentum of this Stream.

It is from our broad view of the *Laws of the Universe* and your important place within it that we can clearly remind you that everything that you want is *downstream* in this glorious Current of creation. And when you relax into the inevitable Well-Being that is your true legacy, you then begin to live life in the way that you had intended before your physical birth.

Just Let Go of the Oars

Most people continually try to calculate the distance from where they are to where they want to be. "How much farther do I have to travel? How much more do I need to do? How much more weight do I need to lose? How much more money do I need?" And this is primarily because, in your physical format, you tend to be *action* oriented.

We would like you to understand, however, that as you begin to approach your world in terms of *vibration* rather than *action,* and in terms of *thought* rather than in terms of *time and space and distance,* your ability to close the gap between where you are and where you want to be will be much more efficient.

Sometimes, even when we are offering analogies such as this one about you in your canoe in the Stream, you want to apply your usual action-oriented tendencies. In other words, often our physical friends accept our premise that what they want is *downstream,* so they want to get pointed in that right direction and then they want to hurry *downstream:* "How can I get *downstream* to the things that I desire faster? I'll focus better. I'll try harder. I will work longer." But we want you to understand that those determined attitudes only cause you to again turn *upstream.* Once you are pointed *downstream* in this Current of Life, it is not necessary to put a motor on your boat in an attempt to make it go faster. The Current will carry you . . . just let go of the oars.

When you are no longer paddling <u>against</u> the Current—when you release your oars and relax into your own natural Well-Being—the Current, which is ever moving in the direction of that which you have become and all that you want, will carry you toward your desires.

The belief that there is something to overcome automatically points you *upstream.* Understanding that all you desire is easily attainable by you automatically points you *downstream.* And once you understand that, you are practicing the *Art of Allowing* your natural Well-Being to flow to you, and you to it . . . and that is the *Art of Allowing* yourself to be the *You* that life has caused you to become.

⋖⋗⋖⋗⋖⋗ ⋗⋖⋗⋖⋗⋖

Chapter Nine

The *Law of Attraction* Needs No Practice

There are three powerful *Universal Laws* that are of value for you to understand if you wish to guide your life deliberately, and the *Law of Allowing* is the last of these. It would seem logical that we would talk of the first *Law,* then the second and finally the third—and we have done exactly that in previous books. We are, however, emphasizing this third important *Law* because it is really the *Law* that you have come here, in this time and space, intending to master. This is the *Law* that you must practice if you are to become the Deliberate Creator that you came forth to be. The first *Law,* the *Law of Attraction,* is not something that you need to practice or even something that you *can* practice, for it is a *Law* that exists in every particle of the Universe—and it just *is.*

Just as your Earthly law of gravity requires no practice but just consistently responds to all matter in a consistent way, neither does the *Law of Attraction* need practice. You do not have "gravity instructors" teaching how to avoid falling up, because falling up instead of down is not an option—or a problem. And, in like manner, you will not need to practice in order to cause the powerful *Law of Attraction* to respond to you in a consistent way . . . for it will bring things to you that match your vibration, and it will do so even in your ignorance of the *Law.*

The second of these three powerful *Universal Laws* is the *Law of Deliberate Creation*. By *deliberately* directing your attention and thoughts toward the outcome that you desire, you can be or do or have anything that you choose. The application of this powerful *Law* has resulted in the manifestation of this magnificent planet upon which you live, and in everything that you are able to see. And in the same way that the Non-Physical *Source Energy* applied this *Law*—and through powerful focus, created this environment that you call life on planet Earth—you are continuing the process of creation from your physical vantage point.

Living the Law of Allowing

And while these first two *Laws* are of extreme importance and your awareness of them is of great value to you and to *All-That-Is*, your understanding and application of this third *Law, the Law of Allowing, is really where all of your personal power lies.*

The *Law of Attraction* says, "The essence of that which is like unto itself, is drawn." And what that means is: If I feel unappreciated because of circumstances that have recently occurred in my experience, the *Law of Attraction* cannot now surround me with people who appreciate me. That would defy the *Law of Attraction*.

If I feel fat and unhappy about the way my body looks and feels, I cannot discover the process or state of mind that is necessary to achieve a good-feeling, good-looking body. That would defy the *Law of Attraction*.

If I feel discouraged about my financial situation, it cannot improve. Improvement in the face of discouragement would defy the *Law of Attraction*.

If I am angry because people have been taking advantage of me, lying to me, dishonoring me, and even defacing my property, no action that I can take can stop those unpleasant things from happening, for that would defy the *Law of Attraction*.

The *Law of Attraction* simply and accurately reflects back to you in a myriad of ways an accurate response to your vibrational output. In short, whatever is happening to you is a perfect *Vibrational Match* to the current vibration of your Being—and the emotions that are present within you indicate that vibrational state of Being.

Once aware of the powerful *Law of Attraction,* many people make a conscious decision to be more in control of their own thoughts, for they have come to understand the power of focusing thought. People attempt to control and more effectively focus their thoughts through a variety of methods—ranging from hypnosis or an attempt to control unconscious thoughts . . . to meditations, affirmations, and strong methods of mind control.

But there is a much easier way of going about the Deliberate Creation of your own experience and of fulfilling your intention for this joyous life experience, and that is an understanding and application of the *Art of Allowing.* It is the conscious, gentle guiding of your thoughts in the general direction of the things that you desire. And as you come to understand this powerful Stream of Life that we are explaining, and as you get a glimpse of the larger picture of *who-you-really-are,* and, most important, as you become convinced that your true work is to simply realign with *who-you-really-are,* the *Art of Allowing* will become second nature to you.

Go with the Flow of Well-Being

And so we will devote this entire book to assisting you in going with the flow of your natural Well-Being. We will discuss the essence of nearly every conceivable situation that you could find yourself in, and we will offer guidance and suggestions that will cause you to turn and go *with* the natural Current. We will help you consciously rediscover the amazing sensory perception that you were born with that helps you determine the direction of your true path. And it is our expectation that as you read this book and return to your conscious awareness of the amazing power of your emotions, you will become the Allower of the Well-Being that you are from your broader Non-Physical, *Source Energy* point of view.

The most common misunderstanding that prevents people from getting control of a situation and gaining their personal balance is the belief that *I need to get to where I want to be <u>right now</u> or as quickly as possible.* We certainly understand your desire to find the answers to your questions quickly or to solve your problems as fast as you can, but still, that urge works against you. When you feel an *urgency* to be somewhere else, you are pushing hard against where you are. That is *upstream*. But an even more important flaw in the premise you are beginning from is this: *In your belief that you must hurry to an improved place, you are discounting the power of the Stream, its speed, its direction, and its promise. And in the forgetting of those things, you are definitely pointed in the opposite direction of <u>who-you-truly-are</u> and all that you have become.*

So now, turn your attention once again to the *upstream/ downstream* analogy, and *feel* for a moment the sensation of *relief* that you would experience if you had been paddling against the Current in an *upstream* direction and then suddenly just stopped paddling, in an attitude of giving in to the Stream and letting it just turn you and take you *downstream*. Let this picture soothe you even further as you try now to remember that this Stream is benevolent and wise, and it is actually taking you toward the things that you want. In your mind's eye, lie back in your boat, feel it turn naturally *downstream,* and relax into the idea that this Stream will carry you to your inevitable Well-Being and to a fulfillment of your desires.

You Are Adding Power to the Stream

The following pages of this book have the potential to help you quickly align with everything you have ever wanted. But that alignment will not be likely unless you have taken the time to accept the validity of the analogy of the Stream.

If you can accept that from your Non-Physical vantage point before your physical birth, you had set forth intentions, and those intentions account for part of the momentum of the Stream . . . and that as you are here in this physical body, life causes you to ask for more things, and that those things account for part of the momentum of the Stream . . . and that in all that you have lived, you are constantly shooting vibrational rockets out ahead of you, and that those rockets account for part of the momentum of the Stream . . . and, most of all, if you can accept that your *Inner Being,* the *Source* within you, now stands in vibrational alignment with all of that becoming, and that the *Law of Attraction* is drawing to that furthermost summoning point . . . *now* you understand the power of this Stream.

So now, before you read further, just lie back for a moment and contemplate this wonderful, powerful Stream of Well-Being, which moves unendingly in the direction of your becoming, and toward the fulfillment of that which is you. . . .

And now you are ready to apply the *upstream/downstream* comparison toward any and all aspects of your own life experience. It is our expectation that you are now ready to personally acknowledge, thought by thought, if you are pointed *upstream* or *downstream;* and whether you are closing the gap between you and You or are holding yourself unnaturally apart.

PART II

Demonstrating the Astonishing Power of Emotions

Some Examples to Help You
Let Go of the Oars

In the pages that follow, we will offer examples on a variety of subjects in which people often find themselves out of alignment with their own desires. We will discuss desires relating to your physical body, your relationships, your life purpose, your financial employment, and even world events. We have gathered these examples from the vibration of Mass Consciousness as you have been living your lives and, in doing so, have been continually asking for improvement and expansion.

Some of these examples will dovetail with things that are important to you right now, and some of them you may not relate to in any personal way, but it will be helpful for you to read them, even if they are not about "your" issue, because within these examples you will find a complete understanding of the *Science of Deliberate Creation.*

It is likely that as you read these examples, you will take issue with some of them, for you may not believe that some of the desires are appropriate. Depending upon what you are currently experiencing and how you are feeling, you may find some of these examples to be frivolous. For example, if you are frightened about a physical condition and you are reading a section regarding how to improve your relationship with someone at work, you may feel annoyed that we are giving so much attention to something that seems insignificant to you, given *your* circumstances. But even though you may not be able to personally relate to some of the examples that are offered here, we encourage you to read through them anyway, for it is our knowing that in the process of reading these examples, you will come to more profoundly understand vibrational alignment.

We do not seek to guide your desires, for your own life has already accomplished that. It is our desire that the following examples serve as a tool that causes you to allow your own alignment with your own desires.

ఆ ఆ ఆ ಶ ಶ ಶ

Example 1

I Have Been Given a Frightening Diagnosis: How Long Will It Take Me to Find My Solution?

Example: "My body is showing some signs of imbalance. In fact, I'm far enough out of balance that I've received an unsettling diagnosis from an expert, and so now I feel fear."

The fear that you feel is understandable under these circumstances, but still you are feeling it, and fear means that you are pointed *upstream.*

Now, it is easy to lose sight of what your real work is here, for there are many varied opinions about the course of action that you should take. Hundreds of books have been written upon the very subject of this diagnosis that has been given to you, but we want to assist you in removing the confusion about what action you should choose and help you simply determine whether you are pointed *upstream* or *downstream.*

It is easy to clutter the situation further by trying to understand what you should have done differently so as not to be in this situation, looking back for a fork in the road where if you had only chosen differently, you could have arrived at a different place: "I shouldn't have done such and such for all of those years," or "I should have done this instead. If I had just taken better care of myself . . . If I had only taken the time for more regular checkups . . . If I had only listened to my mother!"

But we want you to understand that, at this moment, the only thing you need to consider is: *Am I pointed <u>upstream</u> or <u>downstream?</u>* And if you will let that be your only consideration right now, you can begin moving toward the improved state of health that you desire. In other words, there is nothing to consider other than: *Right now am I turned <u>toward</u> improvement or <u>away</u> from it?* And the emotion you feel will give you the answer.

The exercise of determining if you are pointed *upstream* (away from the desired outcome you seek) or *downstream* (toward the desired outcome you seek) will vary from person to person depending upon how fast your Stream is flowing. For example, if your diagnosis is a serious, life-threatening one and you still have a very strong zest for life, you would feel a very strong pulling against the Current (or a very strong feeling of fear) when you focus upon the diagnosis. But if you are no longer very interested in living your life in this physical body, then the feeling of uneasiness would be much more slight. *So the emotion that you are feeling, in any moment, tells you two things: (1) how fast your Stream is flowing, or how strong your desire is about a particular outcome; and (2) which direction you are pointed in the Stream.*

As we begin processing this example, we would like you to consider that even the idea of "healing" is pointed *upstream,* for it implies an overcoming of the illness. Feel the difference between the idea of "beating the illness" and that of "allowing the wellness."

We will offer some statements that are usually offered in a situation like this. See if you can feel if the statement points *upstream* or *downstream.*

This is a very scary diagnosis. (upstream)

I should have taken better care of myself. (upstream)

This disease is hereditary. (upstream)

The options for treatment aren't pleasant. (upstream)

How did I get here? (upstream)

Why did this happen to me? (upstream)

Example 1

It is likely that as you read the preceding statements, you can easily feel that they are *upstream,* resistant statements, but now consider the following common statements:

> *I can beat this.*
>
> *I'm not going to let this get the better of me.*
>
> *I'm not ready to go yet.*
>
> *I will triumph over this.*

We want you to try to understand that those statements are *upstream,* resistant statements, also, for in each of them you are looking at the thing that you do not want and holding yourself in vibrational alignment with the unwanted rather than the wanted. And, in statements such as all of the above, you are not remembering that in the unpleasant experience of contracting the disease, you have already made a vibrational request for improvement, which your *Inner Being* has already achieved; and your *Inner Being* is standing in that improved place, calling you toward it—and THAT is the momentum of the Stream. . . . Your very belief that you need to overcome this adversity has you pointed *upstream* and away from the solution.

Now see how these thoughts feel:

> *This diagnosis has caused me to ask for even more wellness.*
>
> *The larger part of me, my <u>Inner Being,</u> has already achieved that wellness.*
>
> *I will continue to evolve and ask for more.*
>
> *On a vibrational level, I am at my greatest state of wellness.*
>
> *The larger part of me, the <u>Inner Being</u> part of me, is better now than ever.*
>
> *The <u>Law of Attraction</u> is calling the rest of me toward that improved state, also.*
>
> *The natural Current is moving in the direction of my Well-Being.*
>
> *Any action I choose is less important than my knowledge of this Stream.*
>
> *There is no reason for me to struggle in any of this.*
>
> *My Well-Being is inevitable.*

Those were all *downstream* statements. Now, take some time here to feel the relief in the relaxed, *downstream* nature of those statements.

Whenever you feel relief, you have lessened your resistance; and when you lessen your resistance, you are flowing in the direction of your desire. The physical manifestation of your wellness will not be fully evident immediately, but that is not necessary. For now that you have discovered the art of *allowing* your Well-Being rather than the impulse to *resist* it, your Well-Being must return.

As you continue to attempt to guide your thoughts <u>downstream,</u> in time, that will become your natural inclination; it will come easy to you—and your wellness will return. At first your relief will be sporadic; in time, your relief will be consistent—and then the manifestation will match the relief. <u>Disease is the</u> Law of Attraction's <u>response to resistance. Well-Being is the</u> Law of Attraction's <u>response to allowing.</u>

How Long Will It Take Me to Find My Solution?

Question: "How long will it be before I will begin to see improvement in my physical body? In other words, when can I expect a new-and-improved diagnosis?"

While it is understandable that you might still be asking these questions, as you are longing for a quick resolution to your frightening diagnosis, the questions themselves arise from the premise of experiencing sickness and needing a solution. And so, your questions definitely are pointed *upstream*. They also reveal your lack of understanding about the power of the Stream, its direction, and its ability to take you to the solutions you are seeking. When you ask, *How long before I will see improvement?* you are actually asking, *How long will I be here in this place I do not want to be?* The variation in those words may seem slight to you, but we assure you that the *vibrational* difference is huge.

The only way you will be able to personally know if your words, or focus, are *upstream* or *downstream* is by reaching for a visceral feeling of *relief*. For example:

How long before I will see improvement in my body? (upstream)

Example 1

Now try to find a question or perspective that feels better to you than that. Focus on the way you feel, and try to make yourself feel better with your next statement.

Improvement is natural. (downstream)

All in good time. (downstream)

Now, these may not seem to you like earth-shattering statements, and you may not really completely believe them, but none of that matters. The only thing that matters is that by focusing a little bit, you have made yourself *feel* a little bit better. You did not put a motor on your boat and race instantly to some miraculous healing, but you did stop the resistance—you did release the oars; you did turn in the Stream. You did everything that was necessary, right here, right now.

Occasionally something will happen, you will observe something, someone will say something to you, or you will remember something that causes you to point *upstream* again. However, this is not a problem for you because you are now aware of your position in the Stream . . . so, once again, with a little bit of effort, you can release the *upstream* thought by replacing it with something that feels better.

For example, you see someone who is obviously suffering from a debilitating disease and you notice that the person's symptoms seem similar to your own—however, that individual is clearly much sicker than you are. As you see him or her, you feel fear and you think, *I hope that's not where I'm headed.*

But this time, the *thought* does not have priority within you. Instead, your awareness of the way you *feel* takes priority. And since the way you *feel,* right here, right now, matters to you even more than whatever thought you are contemplating, *you make a decision, at this moment, to improve your feeling.*

I hope that's not where I'm headed. (upstream)

I don't know what that person's story is. (downstream)

That person may be better today than a month ago. (downstream)

I don't know what thoughts are creating that person's experience. (downstream)

That person's experience and my experience are unrelated.
(downstream)

I shouldn't go looking for trouble. (downstream)

I think I'll mind my own business. (downstream)

Again, you are not looking for drastic improvement or life-changing ideas . . . just soft, slight improvement in the way you feel. As many situations occur during each day, and as you are aware of the way you feel while you are in them, and as you insist on getting yourself pointed slightly *downstream*—over and over—before you know it, *downstream* will be your natural tendency. And soon there will be obvious evidence in your physical body of the improvement in the direction of your thoughts.

By focusing upon the improved emotion—which you can achieve in this moment—you lay the vibrational foundation for your physical improvement. *When you try to pin down the specifics of <u>when</u> or <u>how</u> the physical improvement will come, you forestall your physical improvement because you do not know those answers, and so you cause resistance in your vibration. In short, although you cannot achieve an immediate physical recovery, you <u>can</u> achieve an improved emotion. And that is enough!*

Example 2

I Cannot Lose Weight

Example: "I've been overweight for as long as I can remember. There were a few brief times in my life when I was able to force my weight under control through uncomfortable dieting and what felt like deprivation, and through arduous exercise. But none of it was easy, and I wasn't able to maintain the regimen for long, and so the unwanted weight always came back.

"I don't feel comfortable in my clothes and dread shopping for new ones. I stand in front of my closet looking for something to wear, and even though I have some nice things, nothing appeals to me because I don't like the way I look no matter what I'm wearing.

"My body doesn't move well, and I know that I'd feel so much better all around if I could just lose a few pounds, but I feel powerless to do anything about this excess weight, so I'm very discouraged."

Now we want to begin this discussion by reminding you of the most important part of *Deliberate Creation:* Creating is not about making things happen through action. In fact, creating is not about *making* things happen at all. Creating is about *allowing* the thing that you desire to happen, and the *allowing* happens through Energy alignment, not through action.

Sometimes this is a hard thing for you to hear because you know, from your personal experience in life, that action *does* get results. You know that you have been able to shed unwanted pounds by decreasing your food consumption, and there is no question in your mind that the exercise helped, too. And we are not disagreeing with any of that, for it is obvious that action does have a place in the creating of many things. In fact, without action, your society would be without a great many of its things. But when you make action the cornerstone of your Creative Process without considering the vibrational basis of your Being as you are taking the action, you are working under a distinct handicap, for there simply is not enough power in the action itself to compensate for the competing Energies of your misaligned thought.

You may recall a successful experience where someone offered you an idea regarding losing weight, and you felt an immediate enthusiasm toward the idea. Your enthusiasm could be attributed to the power of the belief of the person who offered the idea to you, or it could be that the idea dovetailed precisely with beliefs of your own . . . but it is your *enthusiasm* that we want to call your attention toward.

Your enthusiasm was the evidence that the vibration of your Being was in alignment. And then, remember what happened next: You were eager to take the action—and in taking it, positive results occurred. . . . It is possible to take action because someone suggests it or encourages it or even demands it; and once involved in the action, your attitude can begin to improve. But the deliberate alignment of your vibration, first—which then inspires successful action—is a much more powerful approach to whatever it is you want to create.

During your discouraged moments as you acknowledged that your body was not as you would like it to be, you were launching rockets of desire about what you preferred, and within all of that processing of life—and without realizing it—you have been adding to your Vibrational Escrow. You have created a vibrational version of the new-and-improved physical version of yourself.

We want to help you understand that this is not a flimsy dream floating somewhere in your imagination. This is not a delusional departure from reality. This is a creation in the making, and it is being created in precisely the same way that everything you see around you has been created: The living of life gave birth to the

Example 2

idea or thought—which, in time, with focus, became what you call your "reality."

So the discouragement that you have been feeling is indicating the discord between the continually evolving creation of your beautiful body and the thoughts that you continue to think regarding your body. Your body has been vibrationally evolving, but your old patterns of thoughts, your beliefs (which are only thoughts that you continue to think), are causing a vibrational discord. And under those conditions, successful action cannot be inspired or performed. Under those conditions, all action is harder, yielding little or no results, causing more discouragement still.

The key to bringing your body to a new place is to <u>see</u> it differently from the way it is. It is necessary that you focus upon the body that is coming and distract yourself from the negative aspects of your current physical body, for as long as you are <u>seeing</u> your body as it is, you are contradicting the vibration of the idea of a slender body. <u>You cannot create a new reality while looking at your current reality.</u>

So now that you understand why it has been so difficult to find the inspiration to act and why the action, even when you did offer it, netted you very little results, let us show you some very simple things that you can do that will begin the process of aligning your Energies immediately, for by understanding the *Laws of the Universe,* and by understanding the basis of your creation (which is the simple alignment of vibration), you will now be on your way to the outcome that you desire:

- Your choices, right now, do not include whether you are at your perfect body weight or not.

- You have no choice other than to be at the body weight you are at right now.

- You are going to weigh about the same thing tomorrow as you do today, and the next day, too . . . and so on.

- Changing your body weight right now is not an option.

- Changing your vibrational alignment right now *is* an option—a powerful one.

- Also, you are not, right now, choosing between feeling fabulous or terrible.

- You are not choosing between feeling enthusiasm or discouragement.

- Your choices, right now, are more subtle and more fine-tuned than that.

- You are making the simple choice of feeling a little better or a little worse.

- You can choose an *upstream* thought or a better-feeling, *downstream* thought.

- Those are your only choices: *upstream* or *downstream*.

- But those choices are enough.

For example, imagine you are at an outdoor shopping center. You are moving in and out of many beautiful shops, and there are hundreds of people moving in and out of them with you. These individuals vary in size and shape and wardrobe, but you are predominantly noticing nicely dressed, nicely shaped, beautiful people all around you; and as you see them, you feel self-conscious.

You are now awkwardly aware of what you are wearing, and you are unhappy with the way you look today. You turn to see your reflection in the window as you are walking, and you are extremely unhappy about the way you look. You feel agitated, discouraged, and unhappy, and you are not having a good time on this shopping outing at all.

You have now lost interest in the reason why you came to the mall. You do not feel like shopping anymore. In fact, the only thing that is appealing to you right now is the idea of getting something to eat. There are good-smelling things in the air, and you realize that you are hungry and that you do want a snack. There are several choices within view, and from the fragrances in the air, you know there are more choices nearby. Any one of several things sounds good to you: ice cream, candy, maybe something more substantial such as a sandwich. Actually, all of that sounds pretty good to you right now.

Your urge to find a quiet place to sit while you eat something is

Example 2

becoming quite strong, and while you are trying to fight the urge to follow through on your impulse, it is much easier to just give in to it and get something to eat. As you are standing in line at the ice-cream counter, you notice the slender people waiting in line with you. They are annoying, and as you are annoyed, your urge for the ice cream grows stronger still. . . .

Before we continue with the details of this example, and before we offer guidance to assist you in improving your situation, we want to explain something that most people do not understand and, in fact, have a hard time believing: Whether you gird up your willpower and walk out of the ice-cream parlor or whether you go ahead and select—and eat—a large tub of ice cream, there is absolutely no difference in the effect of one of those actions over the other! Even if we are talking about 1,000 days of walking out as compared to 1,000 days of eating a tub of ice cream, the *action* choice of one or the other makes no difference. *It is not your action that matters; it is your vibration. It is not your action that makes you fat; it is your vibration. It is not what you are doing that makes the difference; it is how you are feeling about what you are doing.*

In the beginning of your vibrational alignment regarding your body weight, you may begin to feel enthusiasm for some changes in your diet, and many would say, "Well, then, I don't see how this approach differs that much from just going on a diet as I've done so many times before." But we would ask you to notice how much easier it is this time in the feeling of enthusiasm rather than the discouragement that you have been acting from before. You will also notice that in this state of improved emotion, you will find an appealing idea, and then another. You will begin to find a sort of rolling out of a continuous path of good-feeling new ideas. You will begin to feel carried along by those new ideas rather than struggling to find them, and, before long, you will begin to see physical results. Of course, upon seeing the physical results, your feeling of enthusiasm will be even greater, and then you are really off and running toward the outcome that you have been seeking.

And as you achieve your desired body weight (and you will), you will say to yourself after the fact, *This time it wasn't difficult, and this time I'll keep it off. And, in any case, I now know what to do, whenever I decide to, about achieving whatever physical bodily condition I choose.*

CONSIDER THIS:

If being slender matches the emotion of happiness . . .

and you were to consistently eat ice cream while feeling happy . . .

you would be a slender person who eats large quantities of ice cream.

If your desire to be slender while you are currently not slender matches the emotion of discouragement . . .

and you were to consistently eat ice cream while feeling discouraged . . .

you would be a fat person who eats ice cream.

If your desire to be slender while you are currently not slender matches the emotion of discouragement . . .

and you were to consistently use your willpower to keep yourself from eating ice cream . . .

you would be a fat person who *does not* eat ice cream.

Some would ask, "Abraham, if being unhappy makes you fat, why are there no fat people in an environment where food is scarce? They are unhappy, and *they* are not fat. They are often starving to death." And we would answer, if you are focused upon the current situation of food scarcity, and you feel fear for yourself and your loved ones, you are a match to what you do *not* want. It makes no difference if not wanting to be fat is the issue that turns your thoughts *upstream* or if the idea of starving to death is the issue that turns your thoughts *upstream*: Your thoughts are still *upstream*—which is resistance to what you desire, whether your desire is *slenderness* or *enough food for your family.*

Being slender matches the emotion of happiness. (downstream)

Being fat matches the emotion of unhappiness. (upstream)

Example 2

Having enough to eat matches the emotion of happiness.
(downstream)

Not having enough to eat matches the emotion of
un-happiness. (upstream)

The key to creating everything that you desire is to find a way to turn to the better-feeling, *downstream* thoughts, even when the current situation does not evoke it from you, and to use your willpower to focus your thoughts in the direction of your desire and *who-you-really-are,* rather than using your willpower to try to produce action against the Current.

So, in the beginning, your thoughts may be something like the following:

I am fat. (upstream)

I don't want to be fat. (upstream)

I'm so tired of being overweight. (upstream)

I don't like how I look. (upstream)

I don't like my clothes. (upstream)

I don't want to shop for clothes. (upstream)

I've tried so many things. (upstream)

Nothing works for me. (upstream)

Remember, you do not have to fix everything. Just try to find a thought that feels a little bit better:

I wish I could find a way. (downstream)

My feet would feel better for sure. (downstream)

Again, these are not earth-shattering statements, but they do feel better, and therefore they are *downstream*—so your work, for now, is done.

·:|▨|:·

Whenever you find yourself beating the same old drum about your body weight, if you would make an effort to turn your thoughts *downstream* and stay focused upon the subject until you feel a slight turn, in a very short period of time you will improve the vibrational relationship between where you are and what you want, and you will be amazed at the leverage this improved vibration will give to your process. Everything about this will get easier and easier until, in time, your desired body weight will have been achieved.

So now, let us say that you are at work. You have not been focused on your body or your weight because you had things to accomplish and you've been busy at those things. But now it is lunchtime, and as you are walking past the vending machine, you feel an urge to buy a cookie. You put in your money, the cookie drops through the chute, and while you are unwrapping it, the feeling of discomfort comes over you.

"Here I go again," you say, feeling the discomfort washing over you.

But the urge is strong, and you take a big bite of the cookie.

You feel worse still as a strong feeling of disappointment now rises within you.

But this time things are slightly different from ever before because you have some positive momentum going from those statements you have been making about the subject of your weight.

You remember, *It isn't about what I'm doing. It's about how I'm feeling while I'm doing it.* So you pause and look at the cookie, and you make the following statements:

I shouldn't be eating you. (upstream)

You'll only make me fatter. (upstream)

You are delicious, though. (downstream)

And you're not all that big. (downstream)

I could eat some of you now and save some for later. (downstream)

I like having choices. (downstream)

I like making deliberate choices. (downstream)

I like being in charge of my actions. (downstream)

Example 2

If I had stopped to think, I may not have been so quick to put my money in this machine. (downstream)

I'm really making quite a big to-do over eating a little cookie. (downstream)

You're a tasty little cookie. (downstream)

Well, I'm enjoying you, cookie. (downstream)

I'm <u>deliberately</u> enjoying you. (downstream)

And sometimes I'll choose to eat you, and sometimes I'll pass. (downstream)

Right now I'm going to eat you. (downstream)

And I'm going to enjoy you. (downstream)

You have just accomplished something that is rather unusual for you. You are eating a cookie, and you have talked yourself into alignment with yourself and therefore with your desire to be slender at the same time. You are in alignment with You, which is much more significant than anything you are doing—or not doing—with the cookie. And now, a very slender person walks up to the machine, pulls out a cookie, and begins to eat it. And as you watch, you can tell that this person is truly savoring this cookie.

In the past as you watched a slender person eating a cookie, your thoughts would be:

It's not fair. (upstream)

Her metabolism allows her to eat tasty things and still be slender. (upstream)

She's probably unhealthy, and that's the only thing she will eat today. (upstream)

But this time, because of the vibrational work you have been doing, you think instead:

Ah, there is evidence of someone who's in alignment with her desire of eating a cookie. (downstream)

It is all about vibrational alignment. Do not look for immediate measurable physical results. Instead, look for improvement in your mood, your attitude, and your emotions. When you feel better, you are more in alignment—and everything else will follow. It is *Law*.

≈ᢠ ≈ᢠ ≈ᢠ   ᢠᢍ ᢠᢍ ᢠᢍ

Example 3

My Children Fight Constantly, and They Are Driving Me Crazy

Example: "We have two children: a boy, 12; and a girl, 13. They're great kids—they don't get into trouble at school, and they get good grades—but they fight with one another constantly. They don't hit each other or anything like that, but if they're in the house at the same time, they argue and shout and slam doors all day, every day. They have their own rooms, so they don't need to bother each other, but they just seem to irritate each other so powerfully that they're making my husband's and my life miserable. We've tried everything from forbidding them to go near one another to forcing them to spend an entire day together in one room to work it out. I actually hate to see them come home from school."

It is very interesting to contemplate *Deliberate Creation* through the framework of interpersonal relationships, or *co-creating,* as we like to call it. Many people get lost in the maze of trying to sort things out when it comes to getting along with others.

It is virtually impossible to evoke enough long-term changes from another to ever solve your interpersonal relationship. Most people try to evoke change in the other for a while but then either give up or move on. *Asking others to change so that you can feel better never works.*

If we were speaking with one or the other of your children, we would not guide him or her toward asking the other sibling to change. But this situation is more complicated still: You are on the outside of it, so to speak, wanting to effect change between two individuals; and you are already sensing—from the lack of success that you have had and from the variety of attempts you have made at settling their differences—that you cannot control their relationship with one another.

People often attempt to gain control of the behavior of their children; their employees; or the members of their clubs, political parties, or churches by offering *rewards* for good behavior and *punishment* for bad behavior—but we have never seen any beneficial behavioral changes as a result of that. *Rules and punishments that are effected from the outside usually only cause a hiding of the unwanted behavior—or an even stronger defiant offering of it—because people innately understand that they are not here living their lives to please others.*

We often explain that *you are the creator of your own experience,* and that also means that *you are not the creator of the experiences of others. They are the creators of their experiences.* But we certainly understand that when they are creating their experiences under your roof, within the reach of your eyes and ears, their creation does affect yours, and therefore you should have something to say about the way in which that affects you. We also understand how when you observe a pleasing behavior in another, you are pleased; and when you observe unpleasing behavior, you are not pleased. We also understand how that is compounded even more when it is your own children you are observing. *It is our absolute knowing that if you believe that your happiness depends upon your ability to control the behavior of any other, you will never find happiness—for control of others is not possible.*

There are many who spend their entire lifetimes attempting to gain control of another, only to discover that absolute control of another requires the giving up of much of their own freedom as they turn their undivided attention toward that impractical effort that wastes their life experience because it runs crosscurrent to the *Laws of the Universe.*

Parents often feel such a strong need to guide their children that these words are hard for them to hear, for they believe that

Example 3

they have been entrusted with the care and guidance of their children, so they are often looking for the best way to provide them with some guidance. It is our desire that you come to understand that when you take the time to become fully aligned with *all-that-you-are* before you attempt to offer your guidance, your influence is much more powerful. In simple terms, when you attempt to guide your children from your place of anger or frustration because you are out of alignment with You, your influence is flimsy. However, when you offer your guidance while you are fully connected to *all-that-you-are,* it is powerful.

You could find the humor in this if you will try: "My children's behavior makes me feel such frustration and anger that I lose my ability to guide them, and the harder I try, the more futile it becomes." But when you take the time to come into alignment with *who-you-really-are,* you step into that powerful Current that is flowing toward everything that you desire.

Each time you witnessed the discord between your children, you launched a personal rocket of desire regarding their relationship, for from your personal vantage point, they provided you with detailed contrasting experiences, which caused your personal preferences to evolve. And your personal preferences *are* your business. So now your work is simple: *You must come into alignment with your desires.*

The reason why your children's squabbling is upsetting you so much right now is because that behavior does not match the ideal that all of their previous squabbling has helped you create. In fact, even before their birth, while watching the children of other people, you were flowing your desires into your Vibrational Escrow. Even before *your* physical birth, you were making entries into that Vibrational Escrow account. So it is no wonder that, right now, as you witness something utterly opposite of what you have come to desire, you would feel the discord. It is not simply because they are practicing bad habits of behavior that it is upsetting to you. *Your view of them is causing you to flow in opposition to your evolving creation on this subject.*

If you could accept that your discomfort is simply about your vibrational differences (what you are witnessing versus what is in your Vibrational Escrow) and not really about what your children are doing (over which you have no control), you will begin to show yourself that you can choose thoughts that allow you to feel good (no matter what they are doing); and when you accomplish that, your power of influence will be tremendous.

So, as it stands right now:

- You watch the misbehavior of your children.

- You feel bad.

- You think that you are feeling bad because of their behavior, but you are actually feeling bad because you are out of alignment with your own desires.

- So you ignore what your children are doing and utilize your personal ability to focus in a way in which you can feel good.

- And in doing so, you are now fully connected to *who-you-are.*

- And, also, you are a Vibrational Match to the picture of happy children enjoying each other that you have been in the process of creating for a very long time.

- And with all of that alignment going on, you are in your full Connection to *who-you-really-are;* to the resources of the Universe (that creates worlds); to your *Inner Being;* and to the desires that you have set into motion regarding your children, your family, and your life.

- Now your words and behavior are perfectly timed, they evoke less resistance from your children, and effect more positive change.

But you are not creating through words or through your action—you are creating through your personal alignment with the vibration of your own desires.

So when you think about getting your son and daughter to behave differently, you can feel the uphill battle in that. But when you think about guiding your own thoughts, you can feel the possibility of that. Even, in time, the simplicity in that.

So, wonderful things are about to take place in your experience.

Example 3

Not only are you going to feel better right away by deliberately choosing your own thoughts, but you are going to effect behavioral change in your children (with the help of the *Law of Attraction*) without anyone knowing that you are doing it. And, on top of all of that, through the power of your own example, you will teach your children the value and power of personal alignment. *To show someone how to align with Source—in the face of circumstances that do not easily inspire it—is the most valuable guidance that you could ever offer to another. That is the <u>only</u> guidance you ever intended to offer your children: the power to guide their own lives.*

Let us begin the *Upstream/Downstream Process,* and, as always, you begin where you are, for you cannot begin other than where you are.

My children are driving me crazy. (upstream)

They fight constantly. (upstream)

I can't find a way to stop them. (upstream)

They won't listen to me. (upstream)

Someday they'll regret the way they've treated each other. (upstream)

I don't know what to do. (upstream)

I've tried everything I can think of. (upstream)

It is natural that as you begin, your statements would be pointed *upstream*. But remember that your work in this process is not just to state the obvious or to try to figure out what action you could offer to change things; your work is simply to find some relief for yourself in your own thoughts.

Even the slightest feeling of relief is an indication that you have released some resistance. And with much less effort than trying to effect any sort of change of behavior in another, you can release your grip on your oars, and *your* boat will turn in to the *downstream* flow; more statements of relief will begin to occur to you, and, in time, you will be flowing merrily along toward seeing an improvement in the behavior of your children. *Your power of influence, your ability to evoke different behavior from others, is contingent upon your own alignment with your own desires. <u>You must make yourself feel better before you can attract change</u>.*

Their relationship is really between them. (downstream)

They're probably not feeling nearly as much negative emotion about their relationship with each other as I am. (downstream)

If you were able to hold yourself in vibrational alignment with that last statement for a day or so, that would be enough of a shift in your vibration to begin to effect change. But since this last statement has just occurred to you, and it is not the way you usually think about this situation, it is likely that your thoughts will return to the more usual *upstream* thoughts. So, in order to hold your vibrational ground, so to speak, it is helpful to try to stay there longer by reaching for more statements of relief. *The longer you remain in the improved feelings of relief, the more those better-feeling thoughts will attract other better-feeling thoughts, until, in time, you will be in alignment with your own desire.*

They were very cute when they were little. (downstream)

They played very well together for quite a while. (downstream)

It is possible, as you are reaching for some thoughts of relief, that you will come across a statement that you thought would make you feel better, but which actually makes you feel worse. Sometimes in reaching for an improved thought, you only amplify how much you really want something that, right now, you do *not* have. And so, instead of the feeling of *relief* that you were reaching for, you have an even greater feeling of discomfort—but this does not mean that you are losing ground in your *downstream* process.

Remember: *The way you now feel is relative only to the way you were just feeling. So see this as a fluid, flexible exercise whereby you can move anytime in the direction that you choose. Do not lose sight of your objective, which is to find relief, find relief, find relief. . . . If a thought feels worse than the one before it, it's not a problem. Just reach for more relief. And in time—and usually a rather short time—you will find what you are reaching for.*

Example 3

It's normal for kids to fight.

This is part of their deciphering of life.

They have the right to respond honestly to their environment.

They don't like feeling bad any more than I do.

If they <u>really</u> don't like feeling bad, they'll figure out how to stop it.

I'm going to quit adding my negative response to the mix.

I'm going to let <u>them</u> work this out.

It will be interesting to see how this plays out.

I really have been making more of this than it deserves.

It's pretty funny how much I've been making of this.

It feels good to get my perspective back.

These really are great kids.

We're all in this together.

I like knowing that I have the power to control my own feelings.

I like the idea of influencing my dear children to feel better.

I like knowing that they get to choose how they feel.

I love knowing that I get to choose how <u>I</u> feel about how they feel.

Your awareness of your squabbling children has caused you to add to your Vibrational Escrow. Your desires regarding these inter-personal family relationships have evolved tremendously because of your exposure to them; and now, because of your willingness to turn *downstream* in the direction of that evolved relationship, you are flowing toward your ideals.

Not only has nothing gone wrong here—everything is going along exactly as you knew it would as you made the decision to come into this physical body. You came to live life, to identify things that you desire, and then to give your undivided attention to those desires. That is what <u>Deliberate Creation</u> is all about.

❧❧❧ ❧❧❧

Example 4

I Am Totally Disorganized

Example: "I'd like to be an organized person, but I just can't seem to get it together. I have a variety of interests, and all of them bring a certain amount of stuff with them. So my house is so full of things that are interesting to me, to the point that every place I look I see clutter.

"I seem to find the time to think of new projects and gather up more stuff that relates to them, but I don't find the time to put my things in order. I spend a great deal of time just looking for things. Occasionally I set a day aside with the intention of getting it all cleaned up and organized, but I get bogged down almost as soon as I begin because it just feels so overwhelming to clean it up.

"I know that I should throw most of it away, but I can't bring myself to do that for fear that as soon as I release it, I'll need it or want it for some reason. So I just keep gathering, and I'm buried in my stuff. I can't delegate these organizational tasks to anyone else because no one else knows what's important to me. And if someone else *were* to organize it, I still wouldn't know where things are. I know that I need to clean this mess up and get myself organized, but I feel paralyzed."

This is a good opportunity to point out the effect that the *Law of Attraction* has upon you in whatever your current situation is.

You look around at the clutter, which causes you to feel over-whelmed, and because you feel overwhelmed, you are incapable of doing anything about the clutter. So perhaps you can now rec-ognize that your work right now is not to deal with the mess, for you have already acknowledged that you are paralyzed and *cannot* deal with it. *You have to first find a way of improving your emotional state, and once you are feeling better emotionally, you will find a way of bringing the physical things into organization. In other words, you have to deal with the disorganization in your mind first, and then you can deal with the outward manifestations of it.*

I should throw this stuff away.

I must be crazy to have accumulated so much junk.

What was I thinking?

But when I do throw things away, before I know it, I realize that I did really need them.

It gets worse and worse.

I've never been organized.

These statements are all valid, and they are all *upstream* state-ments. And they do represent how you feel. But now, instead of making statements about how things *are,* or about how they *have been,* try to make statements that cause you to feel better. In other words, your goal here is not to make valid declarations of truth about *what-is,* but, instead, to make statements that give you a feel-ing of relief. If you can find some consistent relief about the subject, your Energy will shift, and the feeling of being paralyzed will be replaced with good-feeling action ideas. An improvement in the way you feel means an improvement in the alignment of Energies between you and your *Inner Being: resistance* or *allowing, upstream* or *downstream.*

I've done nothing wrong by pursuing my interests.

It's logical that I would gather materials that support my interests.

Many people have interests or hobbies that appeal to them.

I can remember my enthusiasm upon finding much of this stuff.

Example 4

I can see how my interest in these subjects caused me to find things to support my interest.

That is the <u>Law of Attraction</u> at work.

I don't need to throw <u>all</u> of this away.

There's nothing wrong with my gathering things that interest me.

I'll find a way to store everything and catalog it so that I can find it when I want it.

I don't have to do it all at once.

I've been living with this for a while, and there's no urgency here.

In time I'll figure out what to do with it.

In the same way I enjoyed finding these things, I will also enjoy organizing them.

It is of value to notice that even though nothing has outwardly changed, the feeling of being overwhelmed has lifted because you have focused your thoughts back into alignment with *who-you-really-are.* We want you to know that whenever you are choosing to think unkind thoughts about yourself (or anyone), you are counter to your *Inner Being,* who only feels love for you. When you degrade, scold, or criticize yourself, you are out of alignment with the greater part of yourself, and there are no greater crippling thoughts than those of self-denigration. When you give yourself the benefit of the doubt, you realign with *who-you-really-are.*

Some say that a refusal to look at your own shortcomings is a state of denial that is not healthy. We reply that pointing out your own shortcomings is the greatest state of denial, for it separates you from *who-you-really-are.*

Some people feel criticism for people who look for their own positive aspects, calling them arrogant or self-serving. We reply that to be self-serving is a good thing—for when you care enough to bring yourself into alignment with the greater part of who-you-are, while you have certainly served yourself (and you know that because you feel so much better)—you now are in a position to be of value to others. But in your depression, you are of no value to any other, for you are separate from the Stream of Well-Being from which you offer value.

⋖⋖⋖ ⋗⋗⋗

Example 5

My Former Partner Tells Lies about Me

Example: "I was married for more than ten years, and we have a ten-year-old daughter. Last year we became divorced, and so my ex-husband and I share custody of our child. We live in the same city so that our daughter can move from house to house relatively easily. Also, we have the physical logistics of all of that working pretty well.

"In our divorce agreement, we agreed that our daughter would be at my house during the week and go with her father on most weekends. (She spends some weekends with me, but most with her father; and we take turns sharing birthdays and holidays, regardless of whether they fall in the middle of the week or on the weekend.) She's a great girl and seems to be doing all right with all of this, although when she comes home from being at her father's house, she usually feels out of sorts to me. She's often irritable, and I can tell that something is bothering her.

"It has recently come to my attention that her father often makes negative comments about me, which doesn't surprise me—I don't feel all that great about him either. But he just makes things up. Really, much of what I'm hearing is just pure fabrication, and I'm worried that he's telling these untruths to my daughter in an attempt to drive a wedge between us. I'm afraid that she will believe *him,* and that she and I will grow apart. I want to defend myself, but I don't know exactly what he's saying, so I don't know how to do that. And I also don't know who else he's talking to or what he's telling *them*, either. How can I make him stop doing that?"

Since you were not able to find harmony with this person while you were married to him, we know that it is not really a surprise to you that you are having a difficult time finding harmony after your divorce, but it *is* possible. In fact, if you realize that the time you spent together actually caused both of you to expand in a variety of ways, you could both benefit dramatically from your relationship even though your marriage has come to an end.

What we most want to help you understand is that while your marriage has come to an end, your relationship with this person has not. And it never will. That is one of the most unsettling things that people discover following a divorce or separation from a former partner. In the midst of feeling extreme negative emotion over some situation they are living, they think that the separation from this person will solve the majority of their problems. But most people find little or no improvement in the way they feel about their ex-partner after their divorce. In fact, most work so hard at justifying why the divorce was a good idea that they hold themselves in vibrational alignment with all those things about the relationship that they did not want. So now, even though they are no longer living in the same space, the other's uncomfortable presence remains a daily occurrence even when they do not actually see one another or interact face-to-face. And because their vibration did not change, even though the physical details of their lives together did change, their next relationship is fraught with the same uncomfortable issues as was the last.

Remember that this relationship, uncomfortable as it was, has caused you to evolve, and your *Inner Being* stands, right now, as the vibrational expression of that expanded Being. If you can find good-feeling thoughts and train yourself, through practice, into vibrational alignment with those thoughts, you can benefit from the experience. But only in finding and maintaining better-feeling thoughts can you close that gap and actually be the expanded Being that your life has caused you to become.

Let us begin the reaching for some *downstream* thoughts. Begin where you are:

Example 5

I'm glad that I no longer have to live with him.

I knew almost from the beginning that it wouldn't work.

I don't know why I stayed there for so long.

I'm not surprised that he's still trying to make trouble.

I hate it that I can't defend myself against his lies.

He's so insecure, and I don't think he'll ever change.

I'll never be rid of the discomfort of this relationship.

I'll always be tied to him because of our daughter.

Better-feeling thoughts do not gush from you just because you have decided that you would like to find them because the *Law of Attraction* does not offer thoughts that are far from your active vibration. And since you have been thinking unpleasant thoughts regarding this person for quite a long time, you are not going to suddenly shift into wonderful-feeling thoughts. But that is not necessary. All that is necessary is that you shift a little bit.

All that is really necessary in order to begin turning in the Stream and flowing toward an improved situation is that you discontinue pushing against it. It really is a matter of just releasing, as best you can, the uncomfortable thoughts. Each time you do so, you will feel a bit of relief that will seem to translate into a small amount of *downstream* momentum, making it now more possible to find another thought of relief . . . and so on.

Your goal, right now, is to just stop paddling <u>upstream.</u> Stop trying to defend yourself, or your position, or your decision for the divorce, or your rightness. Stop defending anything—and just float in your boat.

I'm tired of the battle.

I don't want to fight.

Compared to the previous statements that flowed with such hostility, these statements are a big improvement—and so you do feel relief. It is not necessary that you continue in one sitting until you feel even more wonderful. Sometimes just letting go and discontinuing the *upstream* battle is enough . . . but if you feel like it and can continue just a little more, there is value in benefiting from any additional momentum that you manage to achieve.

It's a good thing that we've divorced.

No one is really to blame for that.

It was something that we both agreed upon.

I'm glad that we live close enough that our daughter can easily spend time with both of us.

Things are better now that we're not all living in the same house.

Sometimes, with only that much effort, you can break through into a much-better-feeling place. If that happens, take advantage of it and make even more positive *downstream* statements.

I understand that we'll always have a relationship.

I do want to make the best of our situation.

I don't want to deprive my daughter of her father.

I don't believe that he wants to deprive her of her mother.

I don't believe that I'm a big part of what they talk about.

We've both moved on with our lives.

I want my daughter to feel good about her parents.

I want my daughter to feel good about me.

I even want my daughter to feel good about her father.

There's no reason for us to continue the battle.

I really feel no interest in fighting.

Now, it may seem that we have used words that have avoided the deepest issue of "Her father often makes negative comments about me . . . he just makes things up . . . much of what I'm hearing is just pure fabrication . . . I also don't know who else is he talking to or what he is telling them . . ." and that is accurate. We are deliberately avoiding the most uncomfortable issues in the beginning of the process, for in doing so, it is more likely for you to find relief through your improved thought.

If you are aware of the way you feel and you consistently reach for thoughts that produce the improved emotion of relief, in time even these intense negative emotions will have subsided—

Example 5

not because your ex-husband has changed, but because you have come into alignment with who you have become as a result of this relationship.

When you understand the value of closing your vibrational gap and of allowing yourself to be the expanded Being that your life has caused you to become, you can actually reach a place of adoration of that scoundrel ex who seemingly caused you so much grief. . . . But all of that in good time.

ᴈᴈᴈ ᴈᴈᴈ

Example 6

My Husband Tells Me How to Drive

Example: "I'm a good driver. I've never had an accident, and I do a lot of driving. I don't have the best sense of direction and am not really very good at reading a map, but once I've driven someplace, I usually remember how to get there again.

"My husband and I spend a lot of time together in the car, and he prefers that I drive, but he wants to make all of the decisions about my driving. He is constantly suggesting that I change lanes or that I get out from behind this big truck; he even wants to choose the way I navigate in parking lots. There are so many different choices that could be made while driving, most of which would lead to nearly identical results, that I just don't see why it's that much better to go this way to get out of the parking lot rather than *that* way. And, sometimes, even though *his* approach may be somewhat better, it feels like the mind that's making the decisions isn't the one attached to the body that's maneuvering the car, so I feel constant discomfort as my natural impulses are continually being overridden by *his* instincts.

"I really believe that if he wants to drive, he should be behind the wheel; and when I'm driving, he should let me drive, and that there must be some happy compromise where he occasionally offers a helpful suggestion without overriding all of my inclinations.

"I'm constantly tormented, even in backing out of a parking place, wondering if my natural choice based on how I see the car positioned will mesh with his suggestion. It's not pleasant to drive under these conditions, and probably not safe. I find myself hesitating like a crazy person rather than just moving ahead with the decision that I've made."

It is important to note that the experiences that you are having are those of co-creation. In other words, your husband is not doing this *to* you, but rather, the two of you, over time, have created this scenario. It may have begun during an incident when you really could *not* decide which way to go, and your mate may have had a clear picture of the best course to take.

Often a suggestion from another point of view can be very helpful. However, what is now occurring is that you are feeling so much agitation over the constant suggestions that you are out of alignment with yourself. And in this misalignment, you are acting hesitantly, which makes your mate feel the need to guide you all the more. So it's an uncomfortable cycle of you being out of alignment, so you drive with less efficiency and focus; he wants to help, which makes you more out of alignment, so you drive with less efficiency and focus, so he wants to help. . . . Both of you have not only developed habitual patterns of actions and words, but also of thoughts and feelings about the situation.

From your place of annoyance and frustration, you can find no solution. Your driving cannot improve (and we note that you see no reason to improve your own driving, for you do not believe that your driving is the problem). But you also have no way of soliciting anything else from your mate. And so, unless you change the way you feel about this situation, nothing can improve.

Many people watching this scenario might suggest that you just let *him* do the driving, or that you take separate vehicles, or tell him to mind his own business and keep his ideas to himself. But then, even you acknowledge that there are times when his suggestions are very helpful.

It is not possible to orchestrate or legislate patterns of behavior without introducing a greater hindrance to the situation. In other words, if you were to tell him that you do not want him to interfere with your driving by giving you suggestions, you would deprive yourself

Example 6

of another point of view that you often find extremely helpful. It is not possible to say to anyone in any situation, "I want you to *always* do this or *always* do that." For the sake of simplifying your lives, you often believe that you do want that, but it is truly not practical.

What you really want is to align with your Broader Perspective so that you can receive the benefit of that broader view. What you really want is to be so aligned with the total resources of your Being that you excel in whatever you are doing.

It is our promise to you that when you are in alignment with your Broader Perspective, you are then acting from a place of deftness, clarity, and precision. Your instincts are sharp and clear, and you make good decisions. And even though your mate may still want to play with you in making the best possible choices as you move about in your vehicle, he would not be offering his suggestions to you because of his doubt in your ability, but, instead, in his desire to play and co-create productively.

You have no way of changing your mate. You cannot modify your behavior enough to soothe that, but you *can* come into alignment with You—and when you do, everything will improve.

So, once again, your work is the same. Make your statements from where you are, but make an effort to find better-feeling, *downstream* thoughts upon this topic that align with *who-you-really-are.*

Some say to us, "Abraham, it is annoying, to say the least, that every suggestion you offer is about what *I* need to do. You never suggest that the other people in my life make changes. I don't think it's fair that I'm always the one who needs to make the effort or make the changes." And we understand why it annoys you that our suggestions are always directed at you and the choices that you are making. But you can choose to look at that in either an *upstream* way or a *downstream* way.

I have to do all the changing. (upstream)

I hold the power to affect my own life. (downstream)

When you think that others need to do something differently than they are doing in order to make your life better, you are really in a place of disempowerment, because you cannot control the actions of others. So those thoughts are always *upstream* thoughts.

But when you understand that you can control the way you feel because you can choose the thoughts that you think, and that with practice you can come into alignment with *who-you-really-are*, regardless of the topic, then not only are you in complete control of the way you feel, but your life must unfold in a pleasing way. Those are *downstream* thoughts.

If you try to sort out why your husband behaves in the way he does *(Did he have a bad experience with past drivers . . . does he feel bored if he's uninvolved . . . does he have a control issue . . . am I really such a terrible driver that I evoke this reaction from him . . . ?),* you will make yourself crazy. Things will only get worse. You do not have to understand the things that may have led up to this situation, but you must stop offering the vibration, here and now, that matches it.

Observing *what-is* only perpetuates it. Trying to figure out how it got started only perpetuates it. Taking action while feeling negative emotion only perpetuates it. An improved situation will only come once you have improved the way you feel.

So begin where you are and reach for better-feeling, *downstream* thoughts. Notice the gradual improvement as you make a statement and then try to make the next one even better feeling:

I don't like the way my husband tries to guide my every move while I'm driving.

If he's so sure he has all the right answers, he should drive.

Sometimes he does offer a helpful suggestion.

Since he doesn't have to watch where I'm driving, he can look around for alternative options.

Two heads are often better than one.

He's never unpleasant when I make a mistake while driving.

He isn't trying to make me feel bad.

His suggestions are well meaning.

When we flow together, we really do <u>flow.</u>

It's nice to have an interested partner.

It does feel like we're in this together.

I appreciate his interest.

Example 6

I do appreciate his help.

I'm a good driver.

I'm a good driver with a good helper.

We do make a good team.

Example 7

I Am Not Happy at Work

Example: "I've been working at this company for just under a year, and I do a good job here. It's a small family-owned business, and there are approximately 20 employees working here. Several of the employees are members of the family who owns the company, but most of us aren't part of the family. I'm the newest employee, and I was hired to do specific things, but since the company is small, it's easy to get involved in more than I was originally hired to do. I'm good at what I do, I'm faster than most people, and I really do like working here.

"I'm bothered, however, because I notice that most of my co-workers do far less than they're capable of doing. Everyone sort of holds back from accomplishing all they could do, and I can feel that they resent me when I try to do my best. When I do my best to apply myself, it's as if they think I'm setting a standard that's too high and that they'll now be expected to live up to it, and so I notice that they undermine me in subtle—and sometimes not-so-subtle—ways.

"I like all aspects of the work here, and I can pretty much step in anywhere and do anything that needs to be done, but I notice that most everyone else tries to guide *their* job activities in the direction of the things *they* would rather do, and they continually shift less-satisfying tasks toward me and a couple of other newer employees. I keep thinking I should say something about it, but I don't want to make trouble. And I don't want to be the target of their anger, either.

"I'm thinking about leaving this place and getting another job somewhere else, but I've done that three times now, and I seem to find a similar situation in every job, so maybe all work environments are like this. Also, every time I go to a new place, I have to learn the new environment all over again, make a new place for myself, and start again at a lower wage.

"I don't know what to do. I don't want to leave, and I don't want to stay. I need to win the lottery."

It is of value for you to acknowledge that there is a bit of a pattern happening here where you continue to find yourself in similar work environments. That happens because as you observe things about your present situation (wanted or unwanted), you activate those observed things in your vibration, and so the *Law of Attraction* brings them to you in your next environment—and so on.

Whatever is most active in your vibration is what will continue to occur in your experience. Many people struggle with this idea because they find it difficult not to observe what is happening around them; and the problem with being such a tenacious observer is that when you are observing unwanted things, you are, at the same time, attracting *more* unwanted things. But there are positive aspects to seeing what you do not want: Whenever you see something you do not want, you automatically send a rocket of desire outward, for you always know more clearly what you *do* want when you are seeing something you *do not* want.

So as you are observing those things in your work environment that seem unfair or unjust or inappropriate, you are, in those moments, creating a *Vibrational Escrow* of an improved work environment, and your *Inner Being* has now focused its attention upon those improvements. And, in fact, the negative emotions that you are feeling arise because *you* are still focused upon the unwanted *what-is,* while your *Inner Being* has moved on to the thought of improvement.

So the following *Upstream/Downstream Process* will help you to get into alignment with what you *now* want from your work environment:

Example 7

*I don't think it's right that most people at work do so much
less than their best.*

*It makes me so uncomfortable to see them taking their money
without doing their work.*

*They seem to feel that if they show up for work, they have
earned their paycheck.*

*They seem to feel that they're being paid for being on the
premises whether they actually accomplish anything or not.*

*When I work in the way I believe I should work, I stick out like
a sore thumb.*

*The owners of the company have no idea what goes on in their
business.*

I believe that if they knew, they would fire most everyone here.

When you are having strong feelings about any situation, you will most likely, in the beginning of the exercise, make several *upstream* statements that merely express how you are, in this moment, feeling. Remember that the *Law of Attraction* always shines a spotlight on whatever it is that is most active in your vibration, so it is natural that when you are irritated about something, those irritants are the thoughts that would most readily occur to you. And remember, too, that the purpose of the *Upstream/Downstream Process* is to soften the hold those thoughts have on you and to simply turn *downstream* toward better-feeling thoughts. In time, with focus, your better-feeling thoughts will come to be what has the hold on you, so to speak—and your life will then begin to show constant signs of improvement.

So now, continue to try to find some thoughts that give you a feeling of relief:

*I'm not at a critical point where I need to make a decision
about staying or going.*

*I don't really know what the company owners know or don't
know about their employees.*

*They aren't asking for my opinion, so I'm doing nothing wrong
by not telling them what I see.*

I really know very little about the other people who work here.

I don't really understand the motivation behind their actions.

What others do, or don't do, really isn't my business.

I like the variety in the work I do here.

I can nearly always find something to do that's interesting.

I can make whatever task I'm doing interesting to me.

I'm actually only unhappy here when I'm pushing against something or someone.

I do have the ability to keep myself happily in balance if I decide to.

It's to my advantage to tune out others' opinions of me.

I really have no way of accurately accessing others' opinions of me.

I only have my opinion of their opinions of me.

I can control my opinions if I decide to do it.

Everything that I experience causes me to vibrationally ask with greater specificity for improved situations.

So, actually, everything in this job that bothers me just sets me up for an improved future experience.

How fast I get to that improved experience depends only upon me and the thoughts of alignment or misalignment that I choose.

I can choose upstream thoughts or downstream thoughts—but either way, they are my choices.

Example 8

My Husband and My Teenage Son Do Not Get Along

Example: "I was married before, and I have a teenage son from that marriage. My current husband and my teenage son don't get along at all. They're not openly hostile, but my husband picks at my son constantly trying to get him to do things that he doesn't want to do.

"My son is very bright and rather independent. When he's enthusiastic about something, he always excels, but he wants to do things on his own terms, and he doesn't like to be coached or guided. So it's like a constant power struggle going on between him and my husband, and I feel like I'm caught in the middle.

"My husband has very strong opinions about how children should behave, and he really gets crazy when he thinks that my son is disrespectful of him or of me. I don't agree with my husband's approach to this, yet I want to support him.

"I'm so weary of the battle. I honestly wonder if any mixed families ever really find happiness. Are there any stepparents out there who truly love their stepchildren?"

While it is certainly understandable how unpleasant it feels to you to be caught in the middle of this situation, it could very well help you to finally come to understand something that is extremely important: It can be relatively easy to manage relationships with other people. In other words, as they ask things of you that will make them feel better, and you are willing to do the things that they ask, you can maintain a fairly agreeable relationship.

As long as you meet the demands of most people, they will like you pretty well and—for many individuals, that is the way they manage their relationships. One or the other takes the dominant role. The submissive one submits and the dominant one dominates, and they more or less accept the roles that they have each chosen. (It may be surprising to hear that the majority of relationships are like that to some degree.) But when a third person, who now asks different things of you, is included in the relationship, the basis of your relationship is threatened.

In your situation, you and your son had already established your relationship. And while you may not have realized it, your son had assumed the dominant role and you had assumed the submissive role, which fit your personalities well. Since your son is self-reliant—and to a large degree, self-sufficient—and since his life was working rather well, it did not feel necessary to you that you gain control. But when your new mate entered the picture and now wanted to assume the dominant role, that threw things out of balance.

It is not so difficult for you to please only one person, but when there are two people who each want different things from you, you now must choose which one of them you are going to try to please. And if they should be like most people—who believe that they feel best only when they evoke the response from you that they need—now you have real trouble, for you cannot serve them both. Under those conditions, the more people you are trying to please, the more you are failing at pleasing most of them—and the more uncomfortable *everyone* is.

In some ways it is flattering that they think enough of you to care what you think or how you behave, but it is a trap any way you look at it. *You simply cannot live your life trying to satisfy the prerequisites of other people. And the only chance you would have at any success in such a scenario would be to dramatically limit your relationships. In other words, you would find yourself really only able to serve one master.*

It is our encouragement that you make a new decision, although most likely the people in your life whom you have trained to expect

Example 8

certain behaviors from you will not like your new decision very much. *Decide that from this point forward, you are going to work to find vibrational alignment between you and You. In other words, you are going to do your best to align your current thought with the furthermost expanded version of you, and you are going to leave everyone else—and their opinions—out of the equation.*

This new decision, while disruptive at first, will come to serve you enormously well, because you just cannot stand on your head in enough different ways to please them all . . . and when you try, *you* will be miserable, and you will fail at pleasing them anyway. You must decide to please yourself, in order to align *you* with *You,* to become a Vibrational Match to your own *Inner Being.*

When you are in alignment, then you have the most to offer others, but it will require their decision to come into their own alignment in order for them to receive satisfaction. *Teach them that their happiness is their own responsibility and, in doing so, you will finally be free.*

So, as always, begin where you are, and then make an effort to improve the feeling of your subsequent statements:

My husband and my son don't get along.

I don't think that they like each other at all.

My husband is overly sensitive and heavy-handed when it comes to my son.

My son deliberately makes things worse than they need to be.

So, that is how you have been feeling. Now try to find better-feeling statements. Since this is an issue that comes up often in your life, you will have ample opportunities to address it, and every time you take the time to try to turn *downstream*—even though there may be no obvious evidence of improvement—your personal alignment will have improved. And if you are steady in your determination to come into personal alignment about this issue, your power of influence will have an effect on the situation, and the physical evidence must come. Plus, you gain the bonus of feeling so much better about it even before *they* begin to act differently.

It is really worth noting that a good part of their imbalance is caused by your response to what is going on. Both of them are using you and your reaction as part of their justification for their own "pushing against," and when you omit your discord from the mix, the whole situation will be soothed that much more. In other words, the fire may still be burning, but you will no longer be pouring your gasoline upon it. So continue by reaching for statements that give you some relief:

These are both nice people.

They're trying to find their place in this new family combination.

There are many dynamics involved here, but I don't have to figure them all out.

You could stop there. You *do* feel better. You have actually done your work for now. But if you feel like continuing, you could benefit from the momentum you now have going:

I can see how I've been exacerbating the situation; and as I don't do that, it will begin to improve.

Now that statement may make you feel more uncomfortable than the last few because you are attempting to, once again, take responsibility for their relationship. Only *you* will really know if any statement feels better or worse, so just continue the effort of turning generally *downstream:*

This too shall pass.

My son will eventually go off and live on his own.

This thought may be uncomfortable because you do not want your son to feel unwelcome and then to leave. So reword the statement and make it feel better:

Children want their independence.

Most children want their independence long before they get it.

It is natural for children to push against anyone who tries to rein them in.

Example 8

It is especially natural for children to resent any new person who tries to rein them in.

While this thought gives you relief regarding your son's behavior, it may make you feel worse about your husband's behavior. So now, try to find relief in that:

This is all very new for my husband.

I know he's doing what he believes is best for my son.

He's trying to find his role in this new family.

I can see how I can set the tone in all of this.

When I don't let any of this get to me and I maintain my balance, I'll have a positive effect.

We all want to feel good; and my feeling good, no matter what, has to make a difference.

Feeling good can be contagious.

I've always been good at lightening a mood.

I love being playful.

It's easy to take life too seriously.

Nothing has gone wrong here.

In the broad scheme of things, we're all doing extremely well.

I'm going to enjoy watching the evolution of my desires.

I'm going to enjoy experiencing the benefit of my personal alignment.

I have no intention of controlling anyone, but it's going to be a lot of fun observing my power of influence.

As you practice and achieve consistent *downstream* thoughts, your power of influence is tremendous in comparison with the power of your influence when your Energies are split. The struggle you have been feeling contributed to the clear desire you were setting forth, and by practicing these *downstream* thoughts, you now come into alignment with the expanded version of these relationships.

Example 9

Since My Father Died, I Cannot Find My Balance

Example: "My father died over a year ago, and I still haven't gotten over it. I really don't understand why I feel such grief. I hadn't lived with him for over 20 years, and in the recent past I've rarely seen him—maybe once a year for the last several years, and then only for a brief visit (and even then we didn't really have much to say). We had very little in common, so why would his death be so upsetting to me?"

Even while you are in your physical flesh, blood, and bone body, you are more a Vibrational Being than anything else. While the vibrations that you are offering today could be fresh and new because of what you are currently focused upon, most people carry many residual vibrations from past experiences simply because it is easier to continue the vibrational momentum of a thought than it is to choose a new direction.

For example, if something had been bothering you, and you had been thinking about it for a few days, and then you engaged in conversation with someone who was in agreement with your complaint and so joined you in a lengthy, detailed discussion about it, it would be much easier for the two of you to continue your discussion about this uncomfortable topic than to change the subject. And if others were to join you, they would most likely either be drawn into the same subject because of the intensity that the two of you had amassed, or they would get up and leave the conversation—but it is unlikely that they would be able to introduce another subject that was very far from the discussion that was already under way.

In a similar way, as you are a child, in learning to offer vibrations in response to the environment that surrounds you, you become set in your vibrational ways, so to speak. And because you often remain in those environments for many years—and because your parents often set the vibrational tone in your shared home—you develop patterns of thinking, of vibrating, of responding to life, that you learn in those very early years. And since it is easier to continue the momentum of those vibrations than to change them, most people, even though they eventually do leave the home of their parents, take many of those vibrational habits with them.

While you are probably not aware of it, much of the way you respond to life today has a great deal to do with your very early awareness of physical life. In simple terms, you learned your worldview early on, and since it was easier to continue with it than to change it, your worldview really did not change very much as you moved through time.

Now this does not mean that you agreed with all of the *ideas* of your parents. We actually are talking about *vibrations* that are even deeper than what you would term *ideas.* Concepts such as *stability, safety,* or *Well-Being* were nurtured in your early environment, even if that environment, by the standards of the world, was regarded as substandard. In fact, since all things are relative, your sense of Well-Being in life is deeply rooted in those early vibrations of your childhood. And, at many unconscious levels, you have been keeping those vibrations active as you have moved through time. *Since the Law of Attraction responds to the vibration of your Being, and since your current vibrations have some active patterns that reach far back into your past—you are, in that way, still tied to your past.*

However, you are a multifaceted Being, and you are living a very full and active life now. So while you still maintain that vibrational basis that is rooted in your childhood, your vibrational nature has matured and evolved, such that today you are offering many vibrations that do not relate to your past. And since this has been a gradual evolution, you really have not noticed it, so you continue to reach into the future, aligning with the new thought

Example 9

patterns and maintaining your stability. That is the process of evolution that all Beings experience.

With the death of your father, your attention shifted from your present life to your past. In other words, for a short period of time, you focused upon, you remembered, you pondered, experiences from your childhood. You talked with people you had not spoken to, or even thought about, in years; and in the intensity of those few days, you reactivated your vibrational past, which is not a match to your vibrational <u>now.</u> That is why you feel out of balance.

So, your life has continued to cause you to ask for more (you have launched those continuing rockets of desire into your Vibrational Escrow), and you have done a pretty good job of keeping up with what you are becoming. But suddenly, with the death of your father, as you looked back instead of forward, you definitely turned *upstream*—and that never feels good.

If you are like most people, you have lived some version of the following scenario: You were born. Your life caused you to identify your own desires, but your unique desires were sometimes not found to be pleasing by your parents. They tried to guide you. Sometimes you yielded; sometimes you did not. When you felt strongly about something, *you* prevailed; and when they felt strongly, *they* prevailed—but mostly *you* prevailed, because it was your life, not theirs. But as long as you were doing things just to please them (or anyone), you were out of balance, and then when you did things that matched your own desire, you came back into balance. As time went on, what your parents thought about things became less of a factor in your vibrational balance because you did not discuss things with them as much. You turned your attention to things that did not involve them, and they turned their attention to things that did not involve you.

It is always easier to establish and maintain the balance of your vibration when you are not trying to integrate into the mix what other people want from you. And if you will take the time to bring your vibrations into alignment, then the *Law of Attraction* won't bring people into your experience who are out of alignment with you. But if you are not in alignment with yourself, you can attract quite an interesting mix of others.

It is a common thing for a person to feel relief as they leave one uncomfortable environment, but then, before they establish their vibrational balance, they plunge headlong into another relationship that has similar components to the last. Often, a girl who has a very controlling father will physically leave that environment, only to then marry a very controlling husband. So although the faces and places changed, her overall experience remains the same.

Now, let's consider the vibrational components of your relationship with your father in connection with *upstream/downstream*. While your relationship with your father has changed through time—and your vibrational balance regarding it has continually evolved—you have no choice other than to begin right where you are. It is likely that you will recognize many of the thoughts that will emerge during this process as things that you have thought about in the past . . . things that had been lying dormant, so to speak, that have reemerged now that your father has died.

It is important to understand that the fact that you are feeling emotions around the thoughts now means they are active now. And if the emotions that you are feeling are uncomfortable, that means the thoughts that are causing them are pointed *upstream*. And any *upstream* thoughts are running counter to your natural direction (and the evolution of your Being); so it is very helpful to soften those thoughts, find relief, and get your boat flowing in the direction of *who-you-really-are*. That is your goal with this process:

I feel out of sorts.

I'm truly depressed.

I wasn't ready for the death of my father.

I had no control in that.

I'm sorry I didn't spend more time with him.

Neither one of us really enjoyed spending time with the other.

I don't actually know what he was thinking.

I don't know what he really wanted.

I wish his life could have been more satisfying to him.

These thoughts are a true depiction of how you currently feel, and all of them are clearly pointed *upstream*—and there is nothing wrong with that. Under the circumstances, it is normal. But even

Example 9

so, you are not going with the flow of your Being, so try to find thoughts that give you relief:

> *I always wanted a better relationship with my father.*
>
> *I should have tried harder.*
>
> *I don't know what I should have done differently.*
>
> *We didn't have a bad relationship.*
>
> *I'm not sure we even had what you would call a "relationship."*

Not much improvement yet, but your desire to find relief is growing, and you are gathering a bit of momentum that could pay off, so keep going:

> *Our relationship was what it was.*
>
> *And we are only one facet of each other's multifaceted lives.*
>
> *I wasn't born to live my life for him, nor was he born to live his life for me.*
>
> *Maybe nothing went wrong.*
>
> *Maybe it just was what it was.*

You are feeling better. You have stopped paddling *upstream* for the moment.

> *But, still, I wish I could have . . .*

Upstream. Try again:

> *That was an important basis of my experience, but there has been so much more.*
>
> *I'm thankful for the early basis that my parents provided.*
>
> *I cannot go back and relive my life.*
>
> *I don't <u>want</u> to go back and relive my life.*

Better. Keep going:

There are so many things I could think about.

There are many positive aspects to my life experience.

My past will always be a part of me, but my <u>now</u> is what matters most.

I'm quite happy about the way my life is unfolding.

I did get off to a pretty good start.

There may be different layers of vibrations that will surface, but now you know what to do when they do.

Often, when a parent dies, your own sense of mortality is awakened, and a feeling of *Life is too short* begins to surface. There are endless scenarios that may occur that could cause you to feel moments of discomfort, but your work whenever that happens is to recognize that the uncomfortable thought is *upstream* . . . and now, just reach for a thought that feels a little better.

Often, it is not until the death of a parent that you take the time to bring your vibrations into alignment. Since a very strong basis of your vibrational offering began back then while you were living at home with your parents, it is very common for many patterns of thought that hinder you today to be tied to that period of your life. *Often the death of your parent can be a major turning point in your own life experience if you will take the time to identify those uncomfortable thoughts and turn them downstream into feelings of relief. Years of unrecognized patterns of resistance can easily be released through this process.*

It is our expectation that you will reach the place where not only will you feel better than ever in your now, but you will have established such a clear Vibrational Connection with the Being you have evolved to that you'll be reviewing your childhood and your past through those eyes of Connection—and then your childhood recollections will be the sweet memories you have always wanted them to be:

I had a wonderful childhood.

It was good in so many ways.

I appreciate my parents, who gave me the avenue into this wonderful life.

Example 9

*They provided the avenue and then set me free to create
my own life experience.*

Life is good.

There are many things that happen in life that have the potential of producing strong negative emotions in you as you focus
upon them, and the majority of those things are completely outside
of your control.

*You cannot prevent your father's death, and you cannot change his
personality either. But by developing the pattern of always reaching for
the best-feeling thought you have access to, right now—by caring about
the way you feel and deliberately turning in the direction of your natural
Current—you can live a joyous experience, regardless of the circumstances
that surround you.*

ཀྵ ཀྵ ཀྵ ཉ ཉ ཉ

Example 10

I Am a Teenager

Example: "I'm still in high school. I live at home with my parents, and I think that I'm a pretty normal kid. My grades are okay, and even though I actually hate school, I have lots of things that I'm interested in and have a couple of really good friends.

"My parents scrutinize everything I do to the point that they're driving me crazy. I have to get their permission to do every single thing I do, and they always act like I'm doing something wrong or planning on doing something wrong. And so, I not only never feel good when I'm with them, but I actually dread going home.

"I wish I could just leave home now and live on my own and do what I want to do, but I know that I should finish school and figure out how to support myself before I do anything like that.

"I wish that my parents would just leave me alone. I feel guilty half the time, and I'm not doing anything wrong. What's up with them, anyway? Why don't they just live their lives and let me live mine?"

We could ask you to stand in the shoes of your parents and try to understand their perspective a little bit, and you might get some of the answers to your questions. But you cannot ever really see through someone else's eyes, and trying to see from the perspective of another is not a good idea anyway, for it only serves to add more confusion to the vibrations within you. Of course, others often do have good ideas that you may want to integrate into your own Creative Process, but it is much easier to personally sort out the details of life one by one, including the aspects that match *your* overall intentions, rather than trying, in one fell swoop, to just live life the way someone else does.

That, in a very few words, is what goes wrong with most parent/child relationships: Your parents usually believe that they are much older and wiser because of the life experiences they have lived, and they want you to benefit from the wisdom that they have accumulated over time. Parents are often the first ones to forget that *you* are the creator of your life experience. Because you and your Well-Being have been important to them from the time of your birth, they often see you and your life as *their* creation—and that is where you run into trouble.

Through the living of their lives and the watching of yours, they have launched their own desires relative to your Well-Being and your life, and then they often feel a need to control your behavior so that it matches the vision that they have created of you. If we were visiting with them right now, we would encourage them not to do that, and we would guide them back into their own personal vibrational alignment. But we are not addressing your parents right now. . . .

In the same way that we would want your parents to understand that it is not the job of you, their child, to modify <u>your</u> behavior in order to please <u>them,</u> we are saying to you that you must not ask your parents to modify <u>their</u> behavior in order to please <u>you.</u>

We know that it feels to you as if it is *their* behavior that is causing *your* discomfort, but if you can come to the realization that you do have options about their behavior, then and only then will you discover a sense of freedom right where you stand. But if you believe that they need to change (which they are not likely to do) before you can feel better, then you truly feel trapped—and so the feeling of wanting to run away from it all is certainly understandable.

As you begin to reach for more *downstream* thoughts, you are going to come into alignment with the expansive Being that your life has caused you to become. And as that alignment occurs, you will be clear, confident, eager, and happy. (These are all things that

Example 10

your parents desire for you.) And as you offer those attitudes in greater frequency, your parents will begin to feel better, and they will back off.

Now you may say, "But I'm doing all the work: I'm working to adjust *my* thoughts so that *I'm* coming into alignment, so *I'm* feeling better, so *I'm* behaving in a way that is more pleasing to my parents—and all they are doing is enjoying my changed personality. What about *them* doing something to make *me* feel better?"

Again, if we were visiting with them, we would guide them toward their own alignment, and we would be reminding them that they really have no control over your behavior. But we want you to understand that when you believe someone else must do something different so that you can feel better, you are truly at a disadvantage, for you have no control over what they do. When you understand that the way you feel has only to do with the alignment of your own thought Energy, and you work to bring yourself into alignment—independent of anyone else's behavior—now you are empowered. Now you really are free.

So we do not encourage trying too hard to understand another's point of view—even though that sometimes *does* soothe you—because, in many ways, our attempt at soothing you is not so different from their changing their behavior to please you. And while most people think this is what they really want, it is our desire that you come to understand that under all conditions, that is counterproductive.

If you become dependent upon being able to solicit improved behavior from others in order to make yourself feel better, you are really going about life the hard way. It is limiting at best, and debilitating at worst. When you understand that you can control the way you feel because you can control the *downstream* direction of your own thoughts, now you are continually in alignment . . . now you consistently feel good. You come back into your own power, your power of influence is tremendous, and you thrive all around. We want to also add that *controlling your own direction of thought, which improves the way you feel, is relatively easy, while getting someone else to change their behavior is extremely difficult, if not impossible.*

We are going to describe some situations that might occur and your subsequent responses to them. Then we will show you how to make an effort at turning your thoughts more *downstream.*

You have announced to your parents that you are planning to go somewhere with one of your friends. You know that ultimately your parents will not stop you from going, but you are met with their usual disagreeable sarcasm—not only about your choice of friends, but about your choice of activity. And you think:

How do you know what's of value for me?

How would you know what's fun for me?

I don't think you guys know what's fun.

I'm not sure you've ever had fun.

While these thoughts are understandable given the attitude your parents have projected at you, they are still all *upstream* thoughts.

You don't understand my life.

You don't give my friends a chance.

I don't see you making any effort to understand.

Understandable, but still *upstream.* Do not ask your parents to change so that you can feel better. Try to make yourself feel better on your own:

I don't need you to like my friend in order for me to like him.

Through my own experience, I've shown myself that he's a good friend.

At least you're not actually trying to control my experience.

And once I leave and meet my friend, I'll begin to have a good time.

I guess I can understand that your motives are good and that you do want what's best for me.

You are now feeling better.

Example 10

But I don't think that you have any way of really knowing what's best for me.

That is more *upstream.*

But I can't blame you for trying.
I'm still going to go.
You're not going to try to stop me.
Things could be a lot worse.
I guess I don't have it so bad.

In this process, nothing has really changed in the sense that your parents are still giving you a hard time, and you are still going out in spite of their subtle protest. But because of your effort to try to turn *downstream,* your vibrations are in a better place than usual. And so, as you go out with your friends, you do not feel the usual rebellious feeling surging through you. You feel lighter and freer, and your fun with your friend gets off to a better start. This time, you make no negative comments whatsoever to your friend. You do not look back at the house/home/parents from which you have come. You just step into your current experience with a lighter step, and you have a better time than usual. And so, when the night out is over and you are heading home, you do not dread your return as much as before.

It is possible that your vibration has changed so much that your aligned Energy affected your parents. You may find them both asleep in bed, rather than propped up in the living room waiting up for you. And whether you see any obvious evidential change right now or not, *you did feel better, and that indicates change—and that is enough.*

❦ ❦ ❦ ❦ ❦ ❦

Example 11

My Friend Talks about Me Behind My Back

Example: "I'm in high school, and I have a friend (she's been my best friend as we've been growing up) who, for some reason, seems to be deliberately trying to ruin my life. She acts like she's still my friend when she talks to me, but then I hear things that she has been saying about me from other people. She tells others that I say things that I don't say just to try to get me into trouble with them. The worst part of it is, I don't know who she's talking to about me or what she's telling them, and so I can't defend myself. And now I'm totally paranoid because I worry that everyone I see has heard one of her lies. Why is she doing this, and how can I make her stop it?"

We know you do not want to hear this right now, but we want you to understand that you are asking the wrong questions here. If you spend much time trying to figure out *why* she is doing this, you will only hold yourself in the vibration of it longer and begin to attract more of it, until you may find yourself with more than one friend behaving in this way.

Trying to get another person to stop doing something is truly a futile endeavor, because even if you had the physical strength or clout to demand a behavioral change, in that effort you offer a vibrational output that completely contradicts your true desire, and you only get even more out of balance.

Instead of asking others to change their behavior, your power is in your changing your <u>reaction</u> to their behavior. You have no control over their behavior, but you do have complete control over your reaction to it.

As you give your attention to something, you activate a vibration within you that matches whatever you are focused upon. So if you are focusing upon something that aligns with *who-you-really-are*, you feel good when you focus upon it because the two vibrational aspects of your Being are aligned. If whatever you are giving your attention to makes you feel bad, it means that the two aspects of your Being are out of alignment. As you understand that the alignment within you is all you need to pay attention to, and as you work to maintain that alignment, not only will you feel good more of the time, but, also, more things in your life will go the way you want them to go.

Many people—as they realize that we are asking *them* to do the changing by controlling their *own* point of focus—complain, "But what about the person who's telling the lies? Shouldn't something be done about that? Why are you asking me to adjust *my* thoughts when *she* is the one who's doing something wrong?" The answer to those valid questions is very simple: *If your happiness depends upon changes that others make, then you will never be happy, for there will always be a need for more people to make more changes.*

As you look around, you will see a never-ending number of things over which you have no control. But if you will learn to turn your own thoughts in the direction of your own personal vibrational harmony, you will achieve a personal alignment within yourself. And not only will you feel better in that alignment, but in that alignment, you will be offering a single powerful vibrational signal to which the *Law of Attraction* is responding. And no matter what the intentions of others are—even if their intentions are about you—they will not be able to override the powerful Current of alignment that you have achieved. We like to say that when you are tuned in, tapped in, and turned on to the Source Energy that is truly *who-you-are;* and when that is your state of Being, only that which you consider to be good can be your experience. You simply tune those with negative intentions out of your experience.

When someone is deliberately telling lies about you, it is an indication of their lack of self-appreciation, for no one who is in

Example 11

alignment with their Source Energy would do such a thing. Many would suggest that you do what you can do to help this person feel better, especially since she has been your friend for such a long time. That may very well be something that you would like to do, since you may want her to begin feeling better, but it is important to realize that if you attempt to offer your soothing from your awareness that your friend is out of balance, that you will amplify the out-of-balance aspect of your friend, and things will just get worse.

You must see the positive aspects of your friend in order to help her; and before you can see the positive aspects of your friend, you must be in alignment with <u>who-you-really-are.</u> So the process of reaching for thoughts that provide <u>downstream</u> relief is a process to help you to feel better; and if you will focus only upon feeling better, you will have done all that is necessary and all that you can do—and it is enough.

So begin where you are:

My so-called friend makes things up to deliberately make trouble for me.

I don't know why she's doing that, and I don't know how to make her stop.

She is no longer really my friend.

A friend wouldn't do that to a friend.

Valid and true, but not helpful. Reach for some thoughts that give you some relief:

People tend to believe negative rumors.

I don't know who she's been talking to or what she's actually saying.

This might be true, but you have no way of controlling any of that, so you are only holding yourself in an *upstream,* resistant position by pointing that out. Remember, your objective is to find *relief,* not to restate the existing condition.

She isn't talking to everyone.

If she's constantly negative, people who want to feel good will avoid her.

Many people are able to consider the source even when they hear negative conversation.

People probably aren't as interested in spreading negative gossip about me as I might think.

I'm actually not the center of everyone's world.

This shows slight improvement in the way you feel. Try to benefit from the slight momentum you have begun. . . . This could very well be a wonderful opportunity for you to tune your thoughts to the most positive aspects of the people in your circle of friends. If one of them were to hear one of these negative rumors from your disruptive friend and confront you about it, if you are in alignment with *who-you-really-are,* she would be able to tell right away that you were not part of the rumor. But when you are angry about it and feel defensive, it is not possible to determine if *you* started the rumor or just felt angry about it after you heard about it. Your vibration is the same either way.

If you tune your thoughts to the most positive aspects of the people you know, in time no one would even think of believing that a negative rumor about you had any truth. They would simply say (if they were to hear such a rumor), "That doesn't sound like her. I don't believe she would say that." And they would be right.

I want my friend to feel better.

It's so nice to have really good friends.

Everyone has good days and bad days.

I like knowing that good days can predominate.

I like knowing that the <u>Law of Attraction</u> sorts it all out.

And I like knowing that nothing to the contrary of the <u>Law of Attraction</u> could ever happen.

I like knowing that I can control how I feel.

I'm all right in knowing that I cannot control how others think or feel.

I hope my friend feels better.

I'm not worried about it.

It's all good.

Example 12

I Have So Little Money, with No Improvement in Sight

Example: "My friend called, wanting me to go get something to eat and go to a movie, but I couldn't afford to do it. It isn't just that I don't think I should spend the money; I really *have* no money. I get paid in two more days, but for now I'm broke. I have enough to eat in my apartment—not anything very good, but I have several cans of soup, cereal, some granola bars, and peanut butter and crackers—so I won't starve.

"But I'm so tired of having no money. Some of my friends have more money than I do, and they don't even have jobs—their family sends them money. How sweet that is! I want to go back to school so I can get a better job, but that takes a long time before it makes any difference; and meanwhile, I can't see how I'd be able to work and go to school at the same time. I wish someone would give *me* some money."

Whenever you are in the middle of some very vivid life experience, it is hard not to notice it. It is logical that you would have a keen awareness of how much money you have right now, because your financial situation affects so much of your life experience—many things that are important to you are tied to your financial state. But while we understand that it is not likely that you could just stop noticing the fact that you currently have no money, we do want you to begin to understand that you have options about how you *feel* about your situation. In other words, you could have no money and feel terrified or angry, or you could have no money and find it amusing. Most discover that the way they feel depends upon the circumstances: *If I have no money right now but I will be paid soon, I would feel much better than if I have no money right now and no way of knowing when any will come.*

Most people feel the way they do at any point in time because of their awareness of how things are. When things are going well, they feel good; when things are going poorly, they feel bad—and that is the reason why so many people feel a need to control the conditions around them.

We understand how enticing it is to attempt to control conditions, because through action and effort, you *can* control some conditions, to a certain extent—but when you begin to see your world and your life from the standpoint of *vibration,* and you put more of your effort toward *vibrational alignment* and less toward physical action, you will discover the leverage and power of thought. You will discover what the wealthy and influential people of your world have known and applied throughout history.

Some very good things are happening to you while you are writhing in the discomfort of not having enough money . . . for, from that uncomfortable place of knowing what you do *not* want, you are launching rockets of desire for what you *do* want: You want a greater feeling of security, and you want more money. You want to discover enjoyable activities that can produce revenue for you. You want to be able to afford things and experiences that are pleasing to you. In other words, your current situation is the basis from which you are asking for many things; and those things, because of your asking, are lining up for you even while you are writhing in a state of discomfort.

However, as long as you are feeling the discomfort, you do not have access to what you have asked for. Your discomfort means that you are pointed *upstream,* while the things you are asking for are all *downstream.* You have to find some *downstream* thoughts regarding you and money, and until you do, nothing will change for you. And so, try to find a thought that gives you a slight sensation of relief:

I'll get paid on Friday, and then I'll have some money.

Example 12

There is a sense of relief in that thought, but it may be short-lived because you are so aware of your usual pattern: You get paid and have money for a few days, you spend the money quickly, and then you end up in that uncomfortable place again. And your discomfort is not only about not having enough money right now; it is also about not having enough money to last, or enough money to really live the way you want to live. You may feel unhappy with yourself that you did not apply yourself more diligently earlier in your life, having no college degree yet and no career choice yet, even though friends your age have these things. You may feel resentment that your parents did not provide more support for you once you reached college age, or that your family had no business to include you in, or that you had no inheritance to look forward to. . . .

Often the subject of money has many deep-rooted ties that you must find relief from or you will not allow yourself to turn and flow in the direction of the desires that your life has helped you to identify. In other words, it really is worth spending the time to find relief whenever you are keenly aware of negative emotions, because every time you make the effort, you release a bit more resistance. In time, you can actually become resistance free, even on subjects like money that have so many connections to resistant thoughts and feelings.

Remind yourself that you are where you are—and that is fine. Just plunge into the process from right where you are, making your statements, whatever they may be; and then work to find more relief in your statements in an effort to turn <u>downstream.</u>

I do get paid on Friday, but I'll probably be broke again by Monday.

I don't make enough money to live very well at all.

So, you are where you are. And this is how things are, but you can feel better than this if you will make an effort.

I do have a job.

I don't like it very much.

I didn't have a hard time getting this job, however.

It came to me relatively easily.

I did have, and still do have, other job options.

I do think I could get a better job if I really wanted to.

Here you have a very slight improvement. But that is a very good thing, because even that much improvement opens a door to another level of improved ideas.

This job seemed like a good fit at the time.

Although I wanted a better job, this was, at the time, about all I could really see myself doing.

My ideas of what I would like to do have changed.

I could do better if I wanted to.

Your words in this last sentence are about the same as the last sentence in the earlier grouping; however, this time, you are *feeling* them more. Your *relief* is obvious now.

There are good-paying jobs that I'm capable of getting.

If that guy can earn more money, I can, too.

Everyone has to start from where they are.

There are lots of self-made millionaires.

Look at me, going from no money at all to thinking about self-made millionaires.

Now, nothing has changed today in the amount of money that you have in your possession, but wonderful things have changed vibrationally in the last few minutes. We want you to understand that the difference in the way you felt and the way you now feel is the difference between no money and millions. But it will take more than one exercise to cause a consistent enough change that you will see results. In other words, what you did just now is enough if you could maintain this freer, more secure, even humorous feeling that you have about money right now—but it is likely that the circumstances of your life will get your attention, and you will revert back to your more usual feelings about money.

Example 12

If you will sit with this improved feeling for a while and make a decision that you are going to use it as a *downstream* touchstone, and you will make a consistent effort to turn toward the thoughts of relief that are *downstream,* in a very short time you will train your vibration into alignment with the desires that you have. And then, not only will you begin to consistently *feel* more financially secure, but your actual financial picture will begin to reflect those vibrational changes. There will be a time, not far from now, when you will experience money flowing to you so abundantly and easily that you will find it humorous that you held it away for so long.

Continue reaching for the better-feeling thoughts:

I always have enough money for whatever I want.

I want many expensive and wonderful things.

I now understand that whatever I want is easily available to me.

I have only to identify it and it comes to me.

I now understand the ease that I have seen in the financial situations of others.

I can now remove money from the equation.

When my life helps me to understand that I desire something, the perfect circumstances to achieve it appear before me.

I can always feel which paths for achievement will please me most.

It is interesting to me how many different paths are offered to me now.

There is so much variety, each path nice in a different way, but all leading to the financial success I seek.

So, if you've been following this, by taking your time and trying to find some of the feelings that we were projecting in these foregoing statements, you have come a long way—from a position of no money to financial independence.

You are where you are. It doesn't matter how much or how little money you have in relationship to others—there are no limitations for you. Your own life is helping you to define your current goals; and when you find relieving <u>downstream</u> thoughts, you will achieve them. <u>Universal</u>

Laws support you in this; the *Law of Attraction* will continue to show you the path of least resistance—and the ways in which your life will improve are unlimited.

◌§ ◌§ ◌§ ◌§ ◌§ ◌§

Example 13

I Cannot Find a Mate

Example: "I've been ready to settle down in a relationship for a long time, but I can't find the right girl. In fact, I've dated many people who want me to commit to them, but I don't feel that way about them. Now I'm almost afraid to date anyone because I can't find anyone who really pleases me, and I don't want to hurt their feelings by rejecting them. It was easier when I wasn't looking for anything serious, but now I don't know what to do. If I don't date, I'm not likely to find someone, but dating isn't working out well at all for me either."

When you really want something and you are looking at something that opposes it, you always feel negative emotions. When you really want something and you believe you cannot achieve it, you also feel negative emotions. But if you do not really care about something and you are offering thoughts contradictory to it, you do not mind that so much. In other words, if someone you did not know were to call you on the phone and explain that this would be the last time they would ever call you, you would feel no negative emotions.

When your desire for something is strong, your feelings around it are strong; when you are focused upon thoughts that have you flowing *downstream* toward your desire, you have strong good-feeling emotions. But when you are focused upon thoughts that have you pointed *upstream* and away from your desire, you have strong bad-feeling emotions.

Your desire for a significant long-term relationship has, over time, become very strong, and that is a good thing. And in your positive expectation of things working out for you, circumstances and events will occur that will bring your perfect mate right to you. But what goes wrong with so many people who are now in the position of really wanting their mate to show up is that they try to force the creation of the relationship by fixating on someone and trying to make *this individual* that perfect mate. Then, as they see evidence of things not going well, they lose their *downstream* direction, and things get worse and worse.

If you could establish a less serious, more playful approach to your relationships—not trying to make each of them "the one I am looking for," but instead saying, this is "someone with whom I am having the pleasure of sharing a meal," or "someone with whom I am enjoying a conversation," or "someone I am having a good time with today"—then you wouldn't use this moment in time as your excuse to defy your own intentions and desires, and the Universe would more easily and quickly provide the rendezvous you are looking for. . . . *When you trust the* <u>Laws of the Universe</u> *and the fluid, life-giving, productive Stream of Life, you will find everything you are looking for. But in your belief that you must <u>make</u> it happen through <u>action,</u> you often hold yourself crossways of the Current, and you hold yourself apart from your own expansive desires.*

When you are truly lighthearted about the people you spend time with, you will attract other like-minded, lighthearted people. But if you are seriously scrutinizing all of them to see if they are your dream mate, you will attract other scrutinizers, and you will just continue to disappoint each other.

When you bring yourself to a good-feeling attitude about meeting people, and you are looking forward to going out on a date for the sake of the fun or pleasure you will have today rather than trying to parlay it into a lifetime relationship, you will be much more likely to remain a Vibrational Match to what you really want in a relationship, and then the Universe will more quickly bring your perfect mate.

When you feel tense and worried about finding someone, or when you are worried about a person wanting you while you do not feel the

Example 13

same way, you are pointed in the opposite direction of what you are looking for, and you are a Vibrational Match to the very thing you do not want—and so, the very thing you do not want continues to be your experience.

Sometimes it is difficult to accept the simplicity of this powerful understanding, but it really *is* this simple. If you are having a good time and are feeling good right now on this date even though this person is clearly not the woman of your dreams, *you are pointed downstream toward what you want.* But if you are *not* having a good time on this date because you see that this person is wrong for you or you are worried about this person feeling sad because you will not choose her, you are not pointed *downstream,* and you are not closing the gap.

You must find a way to feel good now—even in the apparent absence of something you want—in order to get to what you want. And even though you may have endless valid excuses for not feeling good right now, we would find a way of minimizing those excuses and of feeling good right now, for until you are able to consistently feel good, you cannot get to where you long to be.

We would make a decision to make every date, every conversation with a potential partner, every thought about a potential partner, every thought about relationships, flow *downstream.* We would practice *relief* until our thoughts naturally turned *downstream.* And then, not only will you be living a refreshingly good-feeling life—not only will other happy people begin flocking toward you so that you can joyously spend time together—but in a very short time someone will easily and effortlessly appear in your experience, and you will both know that you are the answer to one another's desires.

And when that happens, there will be no game playing. Neither of you will tease the other. You won't play hard to get or say "I love you, but I just need you to change this one little thing for me." You will see one another as the perfect answer to the perfect question that you have been assembling for most of your lifetime. And this will be a relationship that serves you both, that fulfills you both, and one that will be expansive and satisfying on an ongoing basis.

Right now, your only goal is to find relief in some *downstream* thoughts. And so, begin where you are and reach for improvement in the way you feel:

It's hard to find the right mate.

Others want me, but I don't want them.

I don't want to hurt their feelings, but I don't want to settle for less than what I want, either.

It is natural that you would start out with *upstream* thoughts, but now try to find a thought that feels better:

I really don't need to make every date an audition for a life partner.

I like getting to know people for many different reasons.

I find the people I date really interesting.

I'm enjoying exploring my options.

My picture of my life partner has grown out of the dates I've had over the years.

Each of them has added to my picture of what I want.

Every experience in life adds to the evolution of our ideas and desires.

I can feel how natural this process is.

I don't know why I've tried to make it so complicated.

Each of these thoughts brings a greater feeling of relief. And a valuable thing is happening: You are queuing yourself up for a whole new cluster of interesting women who will begin flowing into your experience, but these will be different in a new and important way: They, like you, will be exploring, collecting data, and looking for fun and good conversation. They won't be needy and desperate. They will be confident and self-assured and interested in living life. This better-feeling cluster may hold the one you are looking for, or it may lead you to yet another better-feeling cluster . . . but it won't be long before you'll be face-to-face with the face who recognizes you at the same time that you are recognizing her as the one you want. And you will have every one of your past girlfriends and dates to thank for this rendezvous.

◆◆◆ ◇◇◇

Example 14

My Sister and I Are Not Speaking to Each Other

Exercise: "My sister and I had an argument over a year ago, and we haven't spoken to one another since. Sometimes I think I should just pick up the phone and call her, but then I remember how angry she made me when we last talked, and I don't want to take a chance on going back to those angry feelings again. I don't feel good about not talking to her, but it feels a lot better than how I felt back then.

"She started the argument, and then she wouldn't even try to understand my point of view. She's always been stubborn, she always thinks that she's right, and I've always given in to her just to keep the peace. But I'm tired of always having to be the one who gives in, so I just don't call her."

Most people want to be loved. They want to be appreciated, and they want to be understood. But the trouble with those desires is that you cannot control whether someone else appreciates or loves or understands.

We have noticed that it feels every bit as good *to* love or appreciate or understand as it does to *be* loved or appreciated or understood; and the most interesting thing about that is, you have complete control over that. You have the ability to love someone just because you have decided that you want to. And while what they have done may have upset you so much that you do not feel you even want to *try* to love them, we want you to understand that unless you do love them, you will hold yourself out of vibrational alignment with yourself—because, like it or not, your *Inner Being* does love them.

Since they are the subjects of your thoughts, and since you feel horrible when you focus upon them, you blame them for the horrible way you feel. That is reason enough to stay mad at them, for they seem to be the reason you feel so awful. If they would be different, you would feel better, but since they refuse to be different, you think you can't feel better . . . so they seem to hold the power over the way you feel. No wonder you are mad at them: You have given them your most prized possession—the key to your own power.

When you remember that you can control the way you feel, no matter what, you can regain your own power, and then you can come back into alignment with *who-you-really-are.* And when you are in alignment with *who-you-really-are,* it is easier to put *their* actions, words, and attitudes into the proper perspective. Those things are not your business. Even their thoughts about you are not your business.

Even if the hurt from a relationship reaches far back into your childhood, you can, with far less effort than you might think, bring yourself into alignment, because you do not have to go back in time and rethink everything and sort it all out and find remedies and solutions. Your pain, then and now, is always about only one thing: your *now* vibrations, caused by what *you* are thinking, right now, and how those vibrations relate to the vibration of your *Inner Being* and who that part of you has become. . . . *You are one who loves; and when, for whatever reason, you do not love, you are tearing yourself apart.*

We understand that you feel justified in your anger or hatred, whether the subject of your discomfort is your sister, an evil dictator, or someone who loved you and left you . . . but, no matter what, there is simply no justification for anything other than love and appreciation. The price you pay in your discord is far too great a price to pay. *In our view, <u>nothing</u> justifies an <u>upstream</u> disconnection from self.*

Example 14

Usually the more we try to get you to release your long-standing patterns of hatred for someone, the harder you cling to them, reaching for a more vivid justification for the way you feel. Really this is but a product of your discomfort with your disallowance. In other words, when you have felt bad for a very long time and you associate that bad feeling with the behavior of another person, you take it very personally, and you usually feel extremely justified in your attitude. But all of this fury is because you innately understand that you should be feeling good; and when you do not feel good, you take it very, very hard.

When you discover your ability to deliberately turn your thoughts *downstream,* without any modifying of their behavior at all, you will discover the indescribable feeling of relief that only comes through the releasing of resistance. With this understanding of the power of your own mind, you will no longer be looking for someone to love you or appreciate you or understand you—or soothe you, cater to you, or help you—for you will then be fully connected to the resources of the Universe; and in that Connection, you will be completely fulfilled. And then, such an interesting thing happens: *In your Connection with the vibration that is love and appreciation, you become one who is loved and appreciated by many.*

So begin where you are:

If my sister wants to talk to me, she can call me.

I'm tired of always being the one who tries to make amends.

I'm happier when I don't interact with her.

Maintaining a good relationship with her is too much work.

So, you are where you are. Many might argue that your sister doesn't deserve your love, but we are not encouraging this process because of your sister, but because *you* deserve to be in alignment with *who-you-are.* And, if we were talking with your sister, we would tell her exactly the same thing: *Do not come into alignment and discover the feelings of love and appreciation for your sister—do it for yourself.* <u>*While it certainly would be a wonderful world if everyone were to understand this and deliberately achieve vibrational alignment within themselves, it is not necessary for one other person to understand this in order for you to be joyful—for your happiness is dependent on no other.*</u>

Now try to find *relief:*

This anger has been weighing on me for a long time.

It would be nice to be able to just let it go.

I can't even remember the specifics of our disagreement.

I'm sure now that it wasn't important.

If I didn't love her, I probably wouldn't care so much what she thinks.

Maybe I can love her regardless of what she thinks.

I get it that I can't control how my sister thinks.

I also get it that it <u>is</u> possible to control my own thoughts.

I can feel the freedom in really getting control of my own thoughts.

I think I have always wanted that, and that's why I feel such anger when I don't control my thoughts.

I guess it's time for me to stop trying to hold my sister responsible.

We want you to understand that we are not encouraging that you seek alignment and relief in order to then affect your actions. We are not trying to get you to call and make amends with your sister. It is our desire that you make amends with yourself and that you find a way to choose the kinds of thoughts that let you come into complete alignment with *who-you-are*. Then, from that place of alignment, you may be inspired to action. It is always certain that from your place of alignment, your inspired action is always to your advantage, and that from your place of misalignment, your action is never to your advantage.

I feel so much better.

I do love and appreciate my sister.

Maybe I'll call her later—or not.

I don't have to decide right now.

Example 14

Now that you are feeling better, do your best to maintain those good feelings by redirecting your thoughts whenever you slip away from feeling good. In time, these better-feeling thoughts will become your normal thoughts regarding this subject; and by then, circumstances will begin to appear that move you happily to the next logical step.

Sometimes, once you get to feeling better, you want to immediately jump into action in order to bring others up to speed with you and the better-feeling state that you have achieved. But it is best just to bask in the new-and-improved emotions for a while until they are truly stable within you. Then the *Law of Attraction* will take care of the rendezvousing with others and with the orchestrating of circumstances and events. Your work—your *only* work—is to find feelings of relief and therefore to come into alignment with *who-you-really-are* and what you really want.

Example 15

My Mate Controls Me, and I Feel Smothered

Example: "I was so happy to find this person. We're so compatible in so many ways, and I know that we truly enhance the experience of each other. We do everything together, and we're really good at working and living together. We like the same kinds of food and enjoy the same kinds of people, and we have very similar interests. In fact, if we were to fill out one of those compatibility surveys, I'm pretty sure that we would be found to be a perfect match for each other.

"But lately I've begun to feel not free. My mate seems so involved in everything that I do that I can hardly consider going off and doing something without her, and I realized the other day that I'm weary of having to take her point of view into consideration with every decision that I'm making. I just don't feel free.

"I have a friend who's diligently looking for a mate, and I found myself thinking, *You may be better off than you know without a mate.* That startled me, because I've always thought that it was so much better to have someone to share your life with. But maybe we aren't meant to share every moment, every thought, and every idea. I feel smothered."

No matter how intensely intertwined you find yourself with another person, your relationship is affected many times more by the thoughts that are moving around in your own mind than by the other person who is moving around in your house or in your life experience. That is why it is so interesting to us to see people working so hard at controlling one another while working very little on controlling their own thoughts and perceptions—especially since they have no real control over another and they *do* have complete control of their own thoughts and perceptions.

People often believe that they would feel so much better if their mate would just change in this way or that way, but that truly is a backward approach to things. When you say, "I'll feel better if you will make this change in your behavior or personality," what you are actually saying is, "My happiness is dependent upon your willingness and ability to modify your behavior; therefore I am powerless." *The reason why so many people are so very hard on those they live or interact with is because everyone inherently wants to be happy, but they also believe that their happiness is dependent upon things over which they actually have no control.*

In the beginning of most new relationships, things go along rather well, since both of you are predominantly looking for positive aspects in the other. And, in the beginning, both of you are unnaturally forcing yourself to work harder at pleasing the other. But when you behave from the vantage point of trying to please another rather than from the point of personal alignment, you set yourself up for a great amount of trouble, for it is not possible to hold someone else's desires as the center of your attention, because as a creator, you simply are not wired that way.

By trying to please others, you encourage the distorted idea that someone else is responsible for their happiness, which, in the long run, disempowers them and makes them unhappy. We could accurately say that the harder you try to make others happy, the more unhappy they become because they become dependent on behavior outside of themselves over which they have no control rather than being in alignment within themselves, over which they have complete control.

So, by holding your mate as your object of attention—telling yourself how much you love her and how important it is to you that she is happy—and then by trying to control her happiness through your actions, it is no wonder that you feel smothered, because attempting this impossible task requires an enormous amount of your time and attention.

Example 15

Also, in most cases, the more you try to control circumstances in order to enhance the experience of others, the more dependent they become on your behavior, and in time, the more demanding they become. You are innately such independent Beings that the more dependent you become, the unhappier you become. Interesting, is it not, that your intentions were to make another happy, but instead, you have encouraged less happiness?

Your only chance of influencing another to happiness is for you to truly be happy. And the only way for you to truly be happy is to achieve the state of vibrational alignment between you and You. So let us apply that formula specifically to the subject of your desire for your mate's happiness:

SCENARIO 1:

- You want your mate to be happy.

- You observe her and you notice that she is happy.

- Your desire and what you are observing match—therefore you are in alignment, and therefore you feel happy.

SCENARIO 2:

- You want your mate to be happy.

- You observe that she is not happy about something.

- Your desire and what you are observing do not match—therefore you are not in alignment, and therefore you do not feel happy.

SCENARIO 3:

- You want your mate to be happy.

- You observe that she is not happy about something.

- You do everything you can think of to make her feel better.

- She is distracted from her misalignment and feels temporarily better.

- You like that she feels better and now take responsibility for her feeling better.

- She now becomes dependent upon your behavior for the way she feels.

- She gradually loses her sense of independence, which now makes her unhappier.

- And so, you try harder at making her happy—but she becomes even more unhappy because your behavior is offered from the flawed premise that you should, or even can, make another person happy.

SCENARIO 4:

- You want your mate to be happy.

- You observe that she is not happy about something.

- You use the power of your mind to ignore how she is feeling right now, and you fixate on something that allows *you* to continue to be happy.

- She thinks you should be paying more attention to her and that you should be trying harder to make her happy.

- Your happiness is your dominant desire, so you selfishly ignore her unhappy state and remain happy.

- In your success at remaining happy (because you have practiced it a great deal), you remain in alignment with your Broader Perspective.

- Because you are in alignment with your greater resources, your timing is good, your clarity is good, your vitality is good—and you feel wonderful.

Example 15

- Because you are in alignment with your greater resources, you are emitting a strong vibrational signal of Well-Being; and because your mate wants to feel good, and the vibration that you are emitting is all about that, she is influenced, vibrationally, to her own alignment. In other words, because of your self-ish desire to remain connected to your own resources of Well-Being, you were able to uplift your mate to what she wanted as well.

- But this is the most important part of all: *No matter how much alignment you have achieved, and no matter how strong your vibrational signal of Well-Being is, it is the work of your mate to bring herself into alignment with that signal. You cannot do that for another person.*

So what it really comes down to is that you have to love others enough to encourage their alignment, which is the only thing that can make them happy. So, of course, be as loving and nice to the people around you as you can be, but not because you are attempting to fill some void for them through your behavior. Be loving and nice because you are in alignment with *who-you-really-are.*

And here is the most important factor to remember: It is very simple to want to feel good and to practice the directing of your thoughts until you do. It is extremely complicated to try to affect the behavior or emotional state or alignment of another. *Tend to your own vibrational balance, and let the* Law of Attraction *do the rest of the work.*

So start where you are and try to find *downstream* statements:

I feel smothered.

I'm tired of having to consider what my wife wants regarding everything I do.

I wish she'd get involved in something that would take her attention away from me.

So that is where you are. Now, rather than looking for relief by getting your partner to change in some way, try to find relief through your own thoughts:

Regardless of what my partner wants or thinks, I can think my own thoughts.

I do not have to consider her response to my every thought.

A big part of what I feel is because of what goes on in my own mind.

I am free to think my own thoughts.

This stream of thoughts is definitely *downstream,* and you are now feeling better.

My mate isn't really trying to control me.

Our way of living together has just evolved.

It isn't that I actually <u>disagree</u> with her about much of anything.

We're very compatible in many ways.

She has never tried to dominate or control my thinking.

My feeling of being smothered is more about my jumbled mind than anything else.

I can sort out my thoughts if I try.

I'm in control of my own thoughts.

There are endless subjects that I can focus on.

I am free to pursue any interest I decide on.

Now, once you get pointed *downstream,* it is rather easy to continue to find better-feeling thoughts:

I don't have to sort out everything at once.

Our relationship is predominantly very positive.

I'm experiencing no actual confinement.

That smothered feeling has now lifted completely.

If it ever returns, I know why, and what to do about it.

᭢᭢᭢ ᭢᭢᭢

Example 16

I Am Getting Divorced and Feel Lost

Example: "I've been married for ten years, and last month my husband told me that he wanted a divorce. He said that he'd been thinking about it for a long time and didn't see any point in delaying it. I know that our relationship was far from perfect, but I had no idea that he was so unhappy that he would want to leave.

"He moved out into his own place that same week. I tried to talk him out of it, but he'd already come to such a strong resolve before he told me about his decision that I can tell he's not going to come back. I'm trying to get on with my own life, but so many aspects of my life were tied to him: I'm not comfortable seeing mutual friends, I can't stand to go to my favorite restaurants, and even television programs that we enjoyed together bring me pain. I feel lost in my own life."

We are going to begin by saying something that most people in your situation are not ready to hear and do not want to hear—but if you *can* hear this, it will provide a speedy avenue out of your intense pain:

Your grief is the result of vibrational contradiction within you—and you can fix that.

Usually grieving people say, "Well, of course I'm grieving—look at what has happened to me," and, certainly, we understand the correlation between your husband's leaving and your grief. But there is something much bigger going on here than your response to his action right now, even though he is a significant person in your life.

All of your life (and even before your birth), you have been in the process of creating a Vibrational Escrow regarding your significant relationship; and that vibrational creation is detailed, powerful, and real. And so, as you focus today on the action of your husband (or the lack of this relationship), you are pointed *upstream* against an extremely powerful *downstream* Current. In other words, your grief is not only about the departure of this one person, but it arises because you are crosscurrent of a powerful creation, intention, and vibrational reality. When a Current flows this powerfully and you get crossways of it, your negative emotion is very strong.

This intense grief you are feeling is not because this person has left you. This pain is an indication that you and your current thoughts are defying your own very powerful relationship creation that is alive and well and waiting for you in your Vibrational Escrow. We want to shout to anyone who is suffering over the loss of a relationship: *Your relationship—the one you really want, the one that you have been creating and adding to every day of your life, the one that you amended even during the process of the breaking down of this relationship—is still there in your Vibrational Escrow . . . but this pain you are feeling now means that in this moment you are not moving toward it, but away from it.* In other words, your pain is not so much about this person leaving your relationship as it is that your attention to his action has you focused in opposition to the "dream" of a relationship that you have been in the process of creating for a very long time.

When you come into full conscious awareness of how all things are created, and you understand your *Vibrational Escrow* and your *Emotional Guidance System,* which indicates the direction of your current thought, you will never again be held hostage by the behavior of any other.

When someone walks out the door, understand that it is just a person walking out the door. It is not the end of your dream, the end of your creation, or the end of your life. It is just another experience, giving you

Example 16

even more clarity about what you want and do not want. It is another opportunity for you to create an even more pleasing Vibrational Escrow.

Often, as we explain how you create your own reality and that you can be, do, or have anything that you desire, a person standing in your position then asks, "So will my husband come back to me, since he's the one I really want?" Of course it is possible that as you come back into alignment with your Vibrational Escrow picture of the life you want to live, this man and this relationship could be the path of least resistance to get you to what you want. It often happens that way. However, we would like you to realize that as significant as this man feels to you and to your happiness at this time, really this specific person is not relevant.

The only thing that is relevant is that you come into vibrational alignment with your own Vibrational Escrow; and when you do, the Universe must deliver to you the perfect match. In other words, the relationship between you and You is the one you must work on, and when that one is in alignment, all others will fall into alignment as well.

Your mate's departure has caused you to focus *upstream*, but you are strong enough to take those thoughts as they occur, one at a time, and let them turn *downstream*. Even under these intense circumstances, you can do it. And as you do, you will feel so much better, and whatever you want will then become your physical reality.

The predominant thing that goes wrong in the majority of failed relationships is that one or the other (or both) is holding the other one responsible for his or her happiness. Most people say to their partner some version of the following: "I want to be happy. When you do such and such, I feel happy. And so I'm counting on you to always do what makes me happy."

When you believe that your happiness is dependent on what someone else does, you are setting yourself up for much pain, because no other can even come close to offering enough behavior to keep you in alignment. Only *you* can do that through your *downstream* choices. No one else can even begin to understand the Vibrational Escrow that you have amassed. You are literally asking the impossible when you count on the behavior of another to keep you happy.

The lack of freedom that your partner feels—if he believes that your happiness is dependent upon him—is suffocating . . . so much so that, like the majority of people, he leaves the relationship simply in the quest for more breathing space and freedom.

But feel the *downstream* ease you would feel if someone were to say to you:

> I love being with you, and right now I feel wonderful being at your side. And, by the way, I take full responsibility for the way I feel at all times. I have the power to direct my thoughts, no matter what, in ways to keep me in alignment with *who-I-really-am* and feeling good. So you are free to live your life in whatever way appeals to you, and I'll be fine. I love being with you, living with you, and loving with you—but my happiness is *my* responsibility.

A freedom-seeking, joy-seeking partner would thrive inside a relationship like that, for that kind of understanding provides the basis for an Eternal relationship of joy. When two people understand that they can live and love and expand unendingly together, there is never a reason to leave and go someplace else, because the freedom that most are so desperate for is fully present right where they are.

When you come into alignment with *who-you-really-are* and with the relationship that you have re-created, which your *Inner Being* is calling you toward, it is possible that this man will flow easily back into your experience . . . but that really is (and we know you do not want to hear this right now) irrelevant. When you get into alignment and begin to flow consistently *downstream,* it is now possible for the relationship of your dreams to come to you. You will know it when you see it, and it will not matter what specific face is behind it—for everything about it will be a perfect match to what you have spent your lifetime identifying that you want. . . . Every so-called failed relationship you have experienced has helped your Vibrational Escrow to evolve. It is ready for you. The question is only: *Are you ready for it?*

So, start where you are (since you have no other choice), and try to find increasingly better-feeling thoughts:

I have no idea what I'm going to do.

I don't want to get out of bed.

Example 16

I don't want to see my family or friends.

I just want to be left alone.

Those statements of powerlessness and abandonment are clearly *upstream* statements, but that is perfectly normal as you begin the process. It has been helpful for you to make such statements because doing so has amplified within you the vibration of where you are, and the most helpful thing about knowing where you are is that you will be able to feel the improvement in your vibration as soon as you make an effort to find better-feeling thoughts.

I've given a big part of my life to this relationship.

I thought that we made a lifetime commitment to each other.

I always keep my promises.

I would never do what he did.

I don't deserve this.

These statements are a slight improvement. But while they are still laced with your feeling of powerlessness, you are feeling slightly better as you gather your resources to fight back, in a sense—and it is important to note that anything *downstream* is better than a feeling of powerlessness. Others watching you move from a feeling of powerlessness to rage may very well caution you about your anger, but they cannot gauge the improvement in your vibrational alignment. From their perspective, since they do not feel the powerlessness that you are feeling—rage may very well be an *upstream* thought.

But this is your Stream, not theirs, and only you really know which thoughts give you relief and which thoughts do not. It is possible that you may spend a few days, or even weeks, in your rage/revenge mode, but that is not necessary, because when you realize that you do have a choice, right now, as to the way you feel, there is no reason to remain in the uncomfortable place (by comparison) of rage and revenge.

A note worth considering: From your place of powerlessness, the emotion of rage or revenge was *more* comfortable *(downstream)*, but from a place of frustration, the emotion of rage would be *less* comfortable *(upstream)*. It is your work to continue to reach for thoughts and feelings of greater relief and comfort. And so, replacing your feelings of powerlessness with feelings of anger may very well be the next logical step in your *downstream* motion:

> *I don't deserve this.*
>
> *I deserve a partner who wants to be with me.*
>
> *I have no intention of clinging to someone who would rather be someplace else.*
>
> *My life doesn't depend on this person who can't keep his commitments.*
>
> *Life is too short to waste it with someone like that.*

Thousands of books have been written regarding interpersonal relationships as scholars and counselors attempt to point out the appropriateness of various attitudes or behaviors. But what the majority of them miss altogether is an understanding that there is not only one right attitude or opinion regarding any subject, for two extremely important reasons:

1. First, you do not have access to every thought from where you are standing right now.

2. The appropriateness of the thought is only relevant to where you stand right now.

In other words, no one else knows which thoughts are right for you. But *you* know—your *Emotional Guidance System* is telling you.

So now that you have discovered the improved feeling of anger, let us continue to reach for further improvement in the way you feel:

> *In some ways I'm glad it's done.*
>
> *At least we're not screaming at each other now.*
>
> *Now that it's all out in the open, I feel an odd sense of relief.*
>
> *I don't have to figure it all out right now.*
>
> *I'm feeling exhausted.*

Example 16

Notice the relief you are feeling. You have come to a sort of resignation about what has happened and an acceptance of *what-is*. But the important thing to notice here is the lessening of "pushing against." In this lessening of resistance, you are allowing your Stream to carry you—without a struggle—*downstream:*

Things have a way of working themselves out.

I've always been a survivor.

I'll eventually find my balance.

A feeling of hopefulness is beginning to rise within you, and from here it is really smooth floating. Once you manage to *deliberately* bring yourself into a feeling of hope, the power of your dream, and of *who-you-really-are,* will call you forward. You have accomplished a great deal here merely by making an effort to feel better.

Often with big situations such as this, which affect your life in many ways, you may find yourself reverting back into some of those *upstream* thoughts that, for now, you have left behind. You may feel compelled to relate your experience to a friend or a family member; and, in doing so, you may very well reactivate your feelings of anger, or even of depression. However, having consciously focused yourself into a much-improved emotion regarding this subject once, you now possess the knowledge that you can do it again. And as you make your way along, you feel more important to yourself—without needing to defensively recount the details of your personal saga—and so your *downstream* motion toward everything that you desire (which your life has helped you to define) will continue.

Example 17

My Children Have No Respect for Me

Example: "I'm a single parent and I'm raising three teenage daughters who treat me very badly. I'm not sure when things started to go wrong, but none of them seem to have any respect for me at all. When they were little, they were really nice little girls. They sometimes fought with each other, like all children do, but whenever I got involved in the situation and told them to stop it, they listened and usually did what I said.

"But those days are long gone. Now not only do they not do what I ask them to do, but they openly mock me, rolling their eyes and laughing with each other. It's like they've joined forces against me. I don't know how it happened or when it happened, but it's very uncomfortable. When did I lose control?"

Although there is tremendous variety in the dynamics of families in your culture today, there is a basic belief that many parents hold that is contrary to Universal Forces and, in our view, is the reason for a great deal of confusion and family discord. And your last statement hit right upon it: "When did I lose *control?*"

Of course, it is possible to control the behavior of another to some extent (especially a child who is just coming into this world, small and dependent for so many things), but the concept of controlling another or of being controlled yourself is not something that any of you intended when you made the decision to come forth into this time-space reality. You knew, from that broader vantage point, that all things are attracted vibrationally, and therefore it was obvious to you then that all that was required for the creation of anything that you desired was putting your attention upon your object of desire and maintaining that connection until the physical actualization. No control, manipulation, justification, or hard work is required, but only pure, nonresisted attention to your object of desire.

How free and wonderful life is when no one is attempting to control you and you are not attempting to control any other!

You are born with basic instincts, not only for surviving in this environment, but also for *joyous* survival. You have come forth as a powerful creator; and it was your intention, without exception, to explore possibilities to come to your own unique conclusions about what you want, and to create—through the power of your aligned focus—your own reality. So when others step into your experience and proclaim that *they* are the deciders of what you should create, want, think, or do, you feel strong discord within you . . . a sort of rebellion, which is indicating the *upstream* direction of your thoughts.

When you understand the *Laws of the Universe* and the independent, creative nature of your children, it is possible to offer loving guidance that will be well received by them without stepping on their creative toes. When you realize that your children, like yourself, have come forth to create their *own* life experiences, then you will understand why they rebel when anyone tries to take that away from them. For some, the feeling is as intense as if a pillow were pressed to their face, depriving them of oxygen.

Some parents in extreme situations believe that the more a child rebels, then the stronger the control that is offered must be. Some parents are encouraged, by other teachers of parental control, to establish ultimatums and stick to them until the children finally give in and yield their power back over to the parents (a sort of "breaking" of the children's spirits, as in "breaking" a wild horse, causing them to meekly do what the parent is requesting of them). And while we agree that the taming of these children may provide a quieter or more organized household, we do not encourage the breaking of the spirit of anyone.

Example 17

This business of <u>parenting</u> is a very big topic, and people have been struggling for a very long time to uncover the proper way of approaching it. <u>No other relationship sets the tone for the life experience of every individual more powerfully than the relationship between parent and child—for, from that early beginning, people set those first vibrational tones that most then carry with them throughout their entire lifetime to their graves.</u>

This struggle is not new in your culture or environment, and it will never come into alignment until you approach the subject *vibrationally,* through *thought,* instead of through *action* (whether you are a parent of a child or a child of a parent, or both). The thing that most often goes wrong in a parent/child relationship is that the parent, who is troubled in this moment for whatever reason, attempts to direct the child through words and actions. In other words, this parent is not in alignment with the resources of the Broader Perspective and, in this disconnected state, is now interacting with the child—and no good ever comes from that.

Endless scenarios could be written (and have been written) explaining the variety of bad behavior from both parents and children, but every instance of unwanted behavior could be easily resolved if the following all-important premises were understood.

To Parents:

- You have provided your children an avenue into this life experience.

- You are not the creator of your children's experience.

- Your children have more powerful resources for their guidance and wisdom than you.

- You are not responsible for what your children create now that they are here.

- Your children have the resources within them for whatever they desire.

- Your children are Pure, Positive Energy Beings who have come here with great purpose.

- Your children were set into motion long before you gave birth to them.

- Your children have within them a *Guidance System* that is powerful and precise.

- Your greatest value to your children is to assist them in maintaining their Connection to their own Source Energy.

- You cannot assist your child in their Connection to Source Energy unless you yourself are Connected.

- It is not your work to control your children.

- Every struggle, bad feeling, disagreement, argument, or crisis that you experience with your children happens while you are not connected to your Source Energy.

- Your alignment, your Connection with your own Source Energy, is more important than your relationship with your child—*that* is the control you are seeking.

- When you are mad at your children, you are not in alignment with *who-you-really-are*, but the discomfort you feel is your own doing.

To Children of Parents:

- Your parents have provided this wonderful avenue for you into this time-space reality.

- While your parents certainly do want what is best for you, they have no way of knowing what that is.

- You did not come forth to do the bidding of any other.

- You are the creator of your own experience.

Example 17

- You are an extension of Source Energy, and you have come here with great purpose.

- You can tell when you are on your path by the way you feel.

- However, since your parents have been here longer, they will seek to give you the benefit of their wisdom.

- Much of what they have learned will be of value to you.

- Since your parents have been here longer, they are less likely to sense that Broader Perspective than you are.

- When you remain connected to the Energy of your Source, you will always know the appropriateness of anything you are considering or doing.

- Your parents will most likely attempt some measure of control, but you do not need to struggle against that control—for your control is only your own. You control your life and your own reality by offering thoughts that match your broader intentions.

- When you are mad at your parents, you are not in alignment with *who-you-really-are,* and the discomfort you feel is your own doing.

People often get bogged down in the details of their assessment of one another's actions and the rightness or wrongness of those actions, but no real resolutions are ever found in that way. Committees are formed and studies are made in an effort to find the best parenting methods, and opinions on this subject are as numerous as grains of sand at the beach. Methods switch from less control to more control, back to less control, back to more control, but the key to wonderful relationships and productive parenting has been within you all along.

When you offer thoughts about your children and pay attention to how those thoughts feel, you will have your perfect guide to parenting—and to everything else.

So, begin where you are:

I must control my child.

I can't control my child.

My child is uncontrollable.

My uncontrollable child is doomed to a troubled life.

I need to find a way to control my child.

All of these statements feel bad to you *(upstream),* which means your *Inner Being* is thinking very differently about your role as a parent.

If I don't control my child, I will be seen as a bad parent by my child's school.

This statement feels bad because you *can't* control your child, but your child's school is attempting to exercise control over *you*. None of that is a match to your broader intentions regarding your child.

My children have no respect for me.

If they don't respect me, they will not respect other adults, and that will have a negative impact on their entire lives.

You think that the pain you are feeling is because of your children's disrespect for you, but all emotional pain is really about your disagreement with your own *Inner Being*. In other words, your in-this-moment thoughts do not match the thoughts your *Inner Being* has about the subject. It is very common to try to justify a negative position you are standing in, because at deep levels you know that you should be feeling good. So you are going on to explain that your children's lives will be ruined if you do not do something about their disrespect, but your *Inner Being* is not in agreement with *that* logic, either.

So rather than trying to unravel all of the dilemmas of parenthood from the beginning of time by comparing every technique and its apparent results to every other technique, it is our desire that you bring all of this into simple perspective by doing the

Example 17

only thing you do have control over, and that is the alignment of thoughts, vibrations, and Energies within your own Being.

Focus, and comment about this subject while feeling for the harmony of your Broader Perspective. Try to find a *downstream* thought that feels slightly better than the last; and continue the process until you have shown yourself what your *Inner Being*, or your *Source*, thinks about your parental responsibility, about you, and about your children:

> *I hate it when my girls roll their eyes at me that way.*
>
> *They do it right in front of me, and they don't even care how it makes me feel.*

This is what has happened, and you *do* feel bad about it. Now try to find some *downstream* thoughts without asking them to change their behavior, because you have control over *your* thoughts and feelings but no control (as your experience with them has shown you) over *their* behavior:

> *It's not personal—they don't respect <u>any</u> adults.*

This does not feel much better, because you are still concerned about how their disrespectful behavior will impact their future lives.

Now we do not want to spend any more time explaining *why* your thoughts feel better or worse, because it only slows things down and has the potential of taking you off into other uncomfortable directions. *Just make an effort to make yourself feel better by <u>your</u> choice of thoughts.*

This is a good time to remind you, as you try to get your boat moving against the Current, of the difference between getting a firm grip on those oars, and just letting go of the oars and going with the flow. Try to let go of the control of your girls—and see if it gives you any feelings of relief:

> *I've tried everything I can think of.*
>
> *I've read every book I could get my hands on.*
>
> *It's the first thing I think of when I awaken and the last thing I think about before I sleep.*

I don't know what to do.

I give up.

Now focus only upon how you *feel*. Experience the *relief* of giving up . . . of letting go of those oars. Try to remember that there is value in the *relief,* for it means your resistance has lessened. Every bit of discomfort you have experienced in your interaction with your girls has put more specific desires in your Vibrational Escrow regarding your relationship with them and regarding the success of their lives—and just now, in letting go, you began to move toward those desires. So now you have access to other better-feeling thoughts:

I don't have to figure it all out right now.

Maybe it isn't my job to figure out their lives.

There aren't enough hours in the day to sort through the complicated details of my teenager's lives.

I think that I've been spending far too much time trying to do that.

There are other things I could think about.

They are a big part of my life, but I do have my own life.

It feels good to think about giving the subject of my girls a rest.

My girls would probably like that, too.

You are feeling much more lighthearted now. From your current vibrational stance, your very recent negative feelings even feel a little odd to you. You are feeling some slight humor in the idea that your girls will appreciate your lightening up as much as you do:

They won't know what to do if I'm not haranguing them all the time!

It will be fun to see their surprise instead of the rolling of their eyes.

Example 17

My backing off cannot possibly cause a <u>more</u> negative result, since what I have been doing certainly hasn't produced any positive results.

I like the idea of seeing my girls through the loving eyes of my own <u>Inner Being.</u>

Those wonderful old feelings are very familiar.

I remember seeing each of them as perfect, and feeling joyful about their future.

I really do want to return to those feelings about them.

I wonder what time it is . . . they should be home soon.

I'll be glad to see them.

This will be fun.

We are certainly not suggesting that your trouble with your teenagers has now been completely resolved with this short exercise, but you did come into alignment with your Source. And if you will remain determined to find thoughts of relief when circumstances arise that are uncomfortable, these relationships will be transformed.

When your girls begin to catch wind of your willingness to not only *allow* them to create their own reality, but to *encourage* it, the majority of their pushing back at you will stop. It will be as if you have removed the pillow from their faces, and the flailing about will stop immediately. . . . And now you can all get back into your own individual boats and continue your joyous journeys in this wonderful life experience.

Example 18

People Steal My Creative Ideas

Example: "I've been working as a freelance writer for the last two years. I submit my work to a number of different publications, and it's becoming well known. I'm now at the point that I can support my family from my writing, as the opportunities are steadily flowing in.

"Recently friends and colleagues have been sending me copies of things that have been written by other people who are clearly using information that originated in my work. They change some verbiage here and there to try to mask the fact that they're taking it from my articles, but it's obvious that they're doing nothing more than rewording my work.

"First of all, it's really annoying when I think how much of my time and effort has gone into the creation of my work. Second, it's clearly plagiarism, and I don't understand how they could possibly feel good about it. I don't go around looking for what's working for other people and then copy it for my own benefit. Where's their sense of pride?

"But the thing that bothers me most is that they're taking my clearly thought-out ideas and mixing them with concepts that aren't valid, and so they're actually bringing more clutter and confusion than clarity to the concepts. Why don't they just create their own bandwagon?"

You have been collecting data for some time now, and it is natural that you would come to your own personal view of the world, and it is also normal to believe that *your* worldview is the correct one. And so, as you see behavior of other humans on your planet, it is logical that you would compare your worldview with the behavior of others and often come to the conclusion, "I would never do that!" It also activates within you a feeling that you need to control the behavior of others to keep them from doing those inappropriate things.

Wars that are waged with words, and all manner of weapons, continue century after century as humans struggle to sift through the details of human experience in the search for the "right" human behavior and ideology. But you are really no closer today, with the waging of your most recent war, than your predecessors were with the waging of the first war— for there is no one right way of behaving, thinking, or living.

Often humans believe that the objective of life is to discover the right way of living and then to convince (or coerce) all others to conform with it, but that is exactly backward from what you know from your Broader Perspective as well as from the intentions that you held when you came forth into this physical time-space reality. Prior to your birth into this Earth plane, it was never your intention to attempt to diminish the Universe by systematically eliminating one bad idea after another until you would be left with a handful of good ideas, for you understood that expansion is inevitable in this Eternal Universe. And, most of all, you understood that the variety of ideas—both right and wrong—is necessary for the Eternal expansion. We give this to you because we understand the tremendous benefit you will receive when you no longer stand in a place of insisting on the *rightness* of your point of view while adding equal emphasis to the *wrongness* of another's.

No matter how popular, or correct by whatever standards, your point of view is, while you are pushing against others' ideas, you are activating a contradictory vibration within yourself that is preventing you from the benefit of your preferred idea. And then, if you are like most, you blame the others with their opposing views for your own failure to promote your idea of goodness. And the battle continues.

When you remember that you are the creator of your experience and that no one else need agree with your premises, or your intentions, or your behavior in order for you to be able to achieve

Example 18

whatever you set out to accomplish, then and really only then will you truly be willing to allow others to do as they choose.

It is not necessary to come into agreement about anything with the others who share your planet, but it is essential to come into agreement with your own Being. And when you do so, beneficial ideas that will promote the general welfare of everyone and everything on your planet will flow forth from you.

Do not allow the behavior of another, no matter how ill intentioned it may appear to be (from your point of view), to deprive you of the power, clarity, and joy of that which is truly you.

You can waste your entire lifetime attempting to sort out the behavior of others, categorizing behaviors into piles of "right"; "wrong"; "really, really wrong"; "sort of wrong"; "not so very wrong"; "pretty wrong"; "not as wrong as other things"; "almost right"; "more right"; "righter still"; "very, very right," and so on. . . .

And it is not too much different to say, "I would never do such and such a thing." You may not do it because it just wouldn't feel good to *you*. You may already be aware of the Connection between you and your broader Non-Physical *Inner Being*, and so you may very well know clearly which behaviors are *on* your path and which ones are *not*. But you simply cannot accurately achieve the vantage point within others between who they are being, right now, and who the expanded part of them is. You cannot accurately assess the appropriateness of their behavior, no matter what that behavior may be; and whenever you try to decide what another person should or should not be doing, you are off your path.

And that, friend, is really what is upsetting you. It is not about the stealing or the corrupting of your ideas. It is not even the skimming off of your audiences or competition in the marketplace. What is at the heart of your discomfort while you focus on these plagiarizers is your own misalignment with *who-you-really-are*.

"If that person would only behave differently, I would feel better." There is no greater entrapment than that, because not only can you not control them—no matter how powerful your armies become—but it is crosscurrent of your very reason for Being and of your very Eternal nature.

When you discover the factor of relief that is available through your *downstream* intention, you will discover the path to true freedom—freedom from the bondage that comes from trying to control others when your only work is to control the vibration of your own Being.

The best part of this understanding is that no one else needs to possess or apply this knowledge. You can apply it whether anyone else does or not; and when you do, your world will become exactly as you want it to be. And that is the "control" you have been seeking. That is the secret to life that humans have been looking for.

We are going to walk you through a series of statements, each one an improvement from the one before, bringing you back into perfect alignment with *who-you-really-are:*

> *I've spent many years creating and disseminating my life's work.*
>
> *It feels wrong for others to read it, like it, and then change the words only slightly and claim it as their own.*
>
> *I would never do that.*
>
> *I have always done my best to give credit where it is due.*
>
> *Whenever I receive benefit from something, I always acknowledge it.*
>
> *Asking them nicely has no effect.*
>
> *They clearly see life differently than I do.*
>
> *There are copyright laws in place to prohibit this kind of thing.*
>
> *I would have no difficulty proving that they have taken the bulk of their material from me.*
>
> *There are hundreds of thousands of people who are familiar with my work who would back me up on this.*
>
> *I always have that option should I choose to pursue it.*
>
> *I do know that pushing against others, even when I see them as wrong, is never good for me.*
>
> *My own experience has shown me that there is no shortage of resources.*
>
> *It's not my desire to be the only voice that is heard.*
>
> *The more other people are offering uplifting words to this world, the better.*

Example 18

My desire for people to understand is also being fulfilled through the work of others—we are all in this together.

Everyone starts from where they are, and if my work has been part of the basis from which they begin, so much the better.

Nothing makes me happier than to see others finding improvement in their own life experience.

I'm happy that there are so many others who seek to add to the upliftment of this world.

I joyously applaud all others in accomplishing their own desires.

I'm never diminished by the success of someone else, but rather, my experience is enhanced.

I adore this unlimited Universe.

I'm alive with excitement in my understanding that I, too, am unlimited.

I love understanding that all others are unlimited as well.

Example 19

My Mother Has Been Diagnosed with Alzheimer's Disease

Example: "My mother has been diagnosed with Alzheimer's disease, and I'm very worried about her. I'm worried about what life will be like for her and how we'll take care of her. The doctor said she's only in the beginning stages of it, but that it can be a fairly fast-moving illness and that we should prepare ourselves. I have no idea how to prepare for something like this. She has always been a very smart woman who enjoys conversation and discussing ideas. I don't think I can endure watching her lose all of that."

It is helpful to remember, as you observe the experiences of others, that your perspective of their experience is always different from *their* perspective of their experience. In other words, your mother may feel no negative emotion at all as her focus diminishes, while you could torture yourself a great deal over it.

As you see your mother's ability to focus seeming to diminish, you may wish to find ways to bring her back to a more alert state of awareness. Some work hard to try to induce their loved ones to just try harder to focus, offering them games and stimulation in the way you might try to motivate a child to learn something. But these well-meaning people are misunderstanding something very important about the condition of their parents: This disease is a path of least resistance that their parents have created for themselves for a gradual exit from this physical experience, and any efforts to try to hold them here does not help them.

Of course you would feel better if your mother were living a sharp, clear, joyful experience, but you cannot create that for her. Most people never find a way to bring themselves into joyful balance in a situation like this because, for the most part, they depend on finding improved situations before they find an improved feeling. But since they have no way of fixing a situation like this, they usually find no way of maintaining their own personal balance.

"Give me an improved condition, and then I will feel better" is what most people are asking for, but what is really required of you is the ability to maintain your balance and your Connection to *who-you-really-are*, regardless of the conditions that exist. <u>*Unconditional love*</u> is *"maintaining my Connection to my Source—which is love—regardless of the conditions that surround me."*

Your mother, in this situation, has found a way to free herself of the thoughts that were holding her out of alignment with *who-she-really-is;* and in her death experience, she will then experience complete Connection. However, in understanding what your emotions are telling you, and by making a conscious effort to find increasingly better-feeling thoughts, you will come into your full and complete Connection without the need for the Alzheimer's disease or the death experience to bring it about.

So, from where you are, begin right now to bring yourself into alignment without asking your mother to change the conditions of her experience:

> *I can't bear to see my mother losing her grasp on life.*
>
> *She was always so brilliant; I never thought that this would happen to her.*
>
> *But while I see her frustration, it isn't actually more than what she has usually felt.*
>
> *In fact, many issues that have angered her in the past seem to be diminished in importance.*
>
> *The frustration that she shows seems to have replaced the anger that I've so often seen.*
>
> *These days, I often witness a sort of peaceful resignation in her.*

Example 19

It feels as if she has released many of her long-fought struggles.

Her memory is often vivid regarding some things.

She's clearly not suffering with this as much as her loving family is.

I've never thought that my mother would live forever.

I didn't believe that my mother would live longer than I would.

While it's hard to imagine being prepared for the death of one's parent, in some ways this disease is preparing us all.

And, most of all, it seems to be preparing my mother.

When I see it like this, I feel appreciation for this unfolding.

I'm coming to understand that all things are working for our greatest benefit.

At times, things that seem out of balance and not to our advantage actually <u>are</u> to our advantage.

I'm looking forward to remembering that we're always blessed, and that things are always working out for us.

Example 20

My Office Staff
Cannot Seem to Get Along

Example: "I am the owner of a small business with approximately 20 employees. The business is profitable and is continuing to steadily grow, but at times I'm not sure I want it to get bigger. It seems as if the bigger it gets, the more employees it requires; and the more employees I hire, the more trouble they cause. I believe I was happier with a much smaller business that I could tend to myself. I'm so tired of the personality clashes and petty grievances that staff members have with each other. Sometimes I feel more like a parent or a kindergarten teacher than an employer. I wish they would just get along, do their work, and stop causing so much trouble."

As you focus upon your business, your employees, your clients, and your products, it feels to you that there is a great deal to consider, manage, and control. And the more products and clients you add, the more people your business requires to fulfill that. And in all of these details, it is easy to lose sight of the most important part of your personal creation: *The basis of all of this is vibration. Your business was created by virtue of your thought—not your actions.*

Many people feel disagreement with that statement because they believe they are seeing the results of physical effort and action. We certainly do not disagree that you live in a world of action, and that results can be attributed to actions. But when you realize that your vibration plays a far greater role in the outcomes that you are producing than does your action, and you begin to put more emphasis on your vibrations, thoughts, and your emotions, you will discover a powerful leverage of your time and energy that will profoundly affect your outcomes. In short, you will achieve far greater results with much less time and effort.

When you focus upon a problem, you lose your connection to your broader view, and then things begin to quickly bog down. When you remain solution oriented, you maintain access to that broader view, and not only do you then find speedy resolutions to problems, but you also enjoy the steady process of your inevitable expansion.

There can be no future expansion if your present is not asking for further solutions. And your present cannot ask for a further solution without an existing problem. Your present cannot ask for a further answer without an existing question. In other words, the problems you wish to avoid are actually necessary for the expansion you seek. In understanding that, it is possible to achieve a joyful rhythm of creation that can be enjoyed by you and your employees alike.

Since your business—no matter what its structure or product—is an extension of your thought vibration, most of its creation occurred before the physical pieces were assembled. Through your pondering, wondering about, speculating on, and deciding upon ideas, you set your business into motion; and during that thinking process, you offered very few thoughts that were of a hindering nature.

Since everything that exists in your physical form was *thought* first, then *form,* you were able to see your business clearly even before you found a physical structure for it or gathered employees or products; and in that vibrational state, there was little resistance, and so it expanded rapidly. *The greater part of the positive direction of most companies occurs before the physical business comes together; but for most, once the buildings, employees, and products are in place, the positive momentum ceases because most of the creators of the business now begin to focus upon the problems that arise. Most do not remain solution oriented.*

If you can understand that what you are calling *problems* are really only *requests for answers* from a Universe that can provide answers to any questions and solutions to any problems—and that, in fact, those questions and answers and problems and solutions

Example 20

are the process through which all expansion occurs—then you may joyously begin to settle into the perfect unfolding of your own wonderful business.

Rather than viewing what is happening with your staff as petty grievances, you will see them as the opportunities for creation that they really are, and you will come to appreciate the interesting mix of people and ideas that you have assembled.

The key to your business success and to your personal happiness is one and the same: *You must find <u>thoughts</u> that are pleasing to you rather than asking your employees to behave in ways that please you. Regardless of what <u>they</u> are actually doing, <u>you</u> must find a way to be pleased.*

By insisting upon feeling good, and reworking your own thoughts to the point that you do predominantly feel good, you will align with your ever-expanding desires about your business, and the Universe will yield whatever is required for the physical manifestation of those desires. As you look at the range of willingness, abilities, and personalities of your employees, and as you will fixate upon the things you like best from the mix, the Universe will deliver more like that to you. If you focus upon what needs to be changed, the Universe will deliver more like *that* to you.

Nothing brings out the <u>worst</u> in another faster than your focusing upon it. Nothing brings out the <u>best</u> in another faster than your focusing upon it.

Some business owners want to remove themselves from the petty details of their organization so that they can focus upon the bigger picture and grander ideas, and there is certainly value in holding the big picture in mind. But it is not your attention to the "petty" aspects of your business that is bogging you down; it is the focusing on aspects that cause a disconnection in you. If each time you become aware of a "problem," you see it simply as a question that is summoning an answer, the answer will come quickly, and you will have enjoyed the process of expansion. In other words, the details do not bog you down, but your own split Energy does.

If you are able to tend to your own Energy and maintain your connection to your evolving desires regarding your business, more talented people will arrive to tend to any of the details you wish to release, leaving you available to tend to whatever aspect of your business pleases you most.

There is no ending to the expansion of your business or of you. So, begin where you are and reach for the *downstream* thoughts of relief. Since you are beginning in a place of frustration, not hope-lessness or depression, it will be relatively easy for you to come into alignment with your desire for a well-run, good-feeling business and, more important, with *who-you-really-are.*

I'm so tired of trying to deal with personality clashes at my office.

These people physically left high school years ago, but their petty grievances with each other make it seem that they're still there mentally.

There are so many more important things for me to give my attention to.

My staff is important to me.

The Well-Being of my staff is also important to me.

I have always wanted a nice working environment for my employees.

A large part of their lives is spent at work at my company.

It's understandable that they would want things to be comfort-able for them.

When faced with an unpleasant situation, it's normal to have a knee-jerk reaction to it.

Life is about exploring contrast, and that's what they're doing.

By knowing what they don't want, they'll figure out what they do want.

They may not be nearly as bothered by this as I am or as I think they are.

They are getting the work done.

Their happiness isn't my responsibility.

I'm only feeling unhappy because I myself am focused negatively.

I shouldn't ask them to behave differently so that I can feel better.

Example 20

These people who work at my office have so many positive aspects.

When I focus upon the long list of positive aspects, this unpleasant situation disappears for me.

It's my desire that they figure out how to make it disappear for them, as well.

I love providing an environment for expansion as well as for prosperity.

I love these people.

Example 21

My Husband Thinks This Philosophy Is Nuts and Wants No Part of It

Example: "I have been reading about the *Law of Attraction,* and it makes perfect sense to me. And so I try to pay attention to what I'm thinking and saying, and I've been working with some of the *Processes* to better my life, but my husband doesn't believe any of this stuff. It even makes him angry when he thinks I'm deliberately applying one of the *Processes.* And the more aware I am of how the *Law of Attraction* works, the more that the negative things my husband says bother me.

"I wish that he would try to learn this. I feel like if we were working together on it, we could really improve our lives. But since he won't even try, won't my husband's negative thoughts hinder my positive thoughts?"

Others' thoughts have no power in your creation—that is, unless you are *thinking* about their thoughts. *When you think about your husband's thoughts, they become your thoughts, and then they do affect the balance of your creations.*

When your life is intertwined with another, you often feel that you need to agree on everything and "pull together," so to speak, on the things that you are creating, but we want you to understand that you do not need another to "pull" with you, because the Stream of creation contains all the "pulling" power that is necessary.

However, you cannot pull against yourself and get to where you want to be.

The reason why you sometimes feel that you are hindered by another is only because you are pushing against something. For example, let us say that you have a strong desire to move into a new house in another neighborhood, and that your husband says that he wants to stay in your current house. If you were to think only about your new house, your day-to-day thoughts would be a Vibrational Match to your desire for the new house, and in the absence of resistance, circumstances and events would fall into place to accommodate your desire.

However, if you think about your husband's opposite decision, spending time in your own mind justifying why you want the new house and feeling unhappy about his unwillingness to even consider it—then your day-to-day thoughts do not match your desire. You would have, by virtue of thinking about your husband's opposing thoughts, introduced resistance into your vibrational mix, and you would not be currently moving toward the outcome you want. In other words, your attention to your husband's decision would have you pointed in opposition to your own desire. And so, it would feel to you as if he were the problem, when actually the problem would be contained in your own thoughts.

Some would say, "But if my husband would agree with me, then I wouldn't be having these contradictory thoughts." Of course it is easier to feel good when you are looking at what you want to see, and so it is logical that it would be easier for you to line up with your desire if your husband were in full agreement with you. But there is true entrapment in the belief that your creations would go better if everyone around you would cooperate, because in the majority of cases, those around you are not going to focus with you in the direction of your desires, for everyone has their own personal and selfish interests that are getting the bulk of their attention.

The awareness that you do not need the agreement of any other to create whatever you desire is truly liberating. And, when you are no longer including the opposing thoughts of others into your vibrational mix, your power of influence increases powerfully.

As your husband has been living in this house with you, he has discovered things about it that he would like to be improved. Like you, whenever he does not have the space for something, he

Example 21

launches rockets of desire for more space. In fact, we would like you to understand that a larger, improved house is in your husband's Vibrational Escrow as well as your own. But he has been applying his logic to the idea and has determined that a new house would cause a financial discomfort, would take time to find, and would take more time to settle into. In other words, even though he also wants many of the same things you want for many of the same reasons, he is contradicting his desire with his "practical" thoughts. So not only is *your* desire part of the driving force of this Current, but your husband's desire is causing the Current, also. In other words, he is helping in the creation of your new house whether he knows that he is or not.

So now that the two of you have created, in your Vibrational Escrow, this wonderful new place to live, and now that you are no longer using your husband's concerns as an excuse to contradict your own desire (and so are in perfect alignment with your new house), the house must come. It will come to you in a comfortable way that will be easily accepted by your husband.

No one has the power to deprive you of anything. And when you understand that and no longer push against anything, all things that you desire will flow easily into your experience. And, in time, through the power of your example, your husband may very well come to understand that these *Laws of the Universe* are not "nuts" at all, but that they are powerful, consistent, understandable, and applicable . . . and really fun to work with.

It is of great value for you to understand that even though your husband may be approaching life differently than you are right now, his life is working for him just the same. Let him *think* as he thinks, *be* as he is, and *want* as he wants, for in doing so, nothing about him will hinder you. But if you attempt to "reform" him, you will most likely be focused on unwanted aspects—which you will include in your vibrational mix, which will hinder your creation, which could, in time, cause you to resent him for (seemingly) holding you back from your desires.

All other people in your life—friends, strangers, even enemies—can contribute positively to your Creative Process. But you are the one who determines whether they add benefit or detriment, because you are the one who sees them in an <u>upstream</u>, resistant manner or in a <u>downstream</u>, allowing manner.

So begin where you are and reach for improved-feeling, *downstream* thoughts:

Our life could go so much better if my husband would try to be more positive.

These Processes really work for me, but he refuses to even consider them.

If he would just try them, I know he would benefit.

If he would just try them, I know I would benefit.

As I worry about what he's doing, I'm not really applying the Processes.

Even someone as close to me as my husband needn't affect my point of attraction.

We don't disagree on everything.

And while our agreement is satisfying, it's not required for me to get what I want.

I've had the experience of secretly desiring things that did come to pass.

Those wonderful things came to me without my collaboration with others.

I'm powerful enough in my own Beingness to create whatever I choose.

I've been holding my husband in an unfair place by requiring his agreement.

By holding to my ideas of what I desire, I'm in no way pushing against him.

We make a good team because we approach life with a differing view.

It's satisfying to observe the cooperative Universe responding to me.

In time, if he wants, we can openly co-create on many subjects.

In the meantime, I'll silently and joyously create whatever I choose.

Example 21

I look forward to his joyous discovery of these <u>Processes.</u>
I do love him.

এই এই এই ই৯ ই৯ ই৯

Example 22

I Am Considered "Old" in This Society

Example: "I'm in my 70s, and there are a lot of things that I did when I was younger that I no longer do, but I actually don't feel much different than I've felt most of my life. I look different, for sure, but I don't *feel* so very different.

"Recently I've been noticing how many people are making reference to 'age' and to 'old age.' The comedians on television are relentless about the maladies of 'old people,' and I have to say, it's beginning to get to me. I believe that I have many happy and potentially productive years ahead of me, but I'm beginning to feel bad—maybe even depressed—about my age."

We find it humorous to hear an Eternal Being speaking of the shortness of life, but of course we understand that you are not seeing yourself in the full, broad view in which *we* see you. The awareness that most humans have of themselves usually extends only from their physical entrance into this body to their physical exit from this body; and the longer they live and the closer to that exit they think they are, the more uncomfortable they become. If they only knew that that exit is but another entrance, their discomfort would be replaced with a delicious sense of Eternal adventure.

We can talk all day, every day, about the Eternal nature of your Being, but of course, you only see what you see. And this time-space reality in which you are focused is an environment that is so vividly focused that you call it "real life," as if to say that the Non-Physical part of it, including us, is not real.

As you deliberately reach for better-feeling thoughts in an effort to apply our repetitive *downstream/upstream* analogy, you will eventually tune the vibration of your physical Being to your own Broader Perspective. And as you do that, the lines of your physical entrances and exits will become blurred and nonimportant as you don your broader Eternal persona. When you are joyously focused in your current moment in time—allowing the broader part of you to flow through you completely and exploring this *now* moment for nuggets of pleasing life experience—all feelings of lack will disappear as your Eternal nature dominates. Your current moment will be so delicious and compelling that there will be no time or interest to look longingly toward the past or feel the shortness of any future. You will begin to recognize that you will be alive and living life for Eternity.

You have no idea how very "old" you are. But you do feel as you feel, and you are the only one who can do anything about that. And the best part of this subject is that there really is nothing that you can do—in terms of action—to change this. You cannot fix it by demanding a behavioral adjustment from another or by turning back the calendar yourself. But you *can* find a way of approaching the subject of your age in a way that brings you into alignment with your Broader Perspective; and when you do, not only will you feel better immediately, but the rest of your physical experience will be filled with wonder and delight.

So, begin where you are and reach for increasingly better-feeling thoughts:

I hate the fun the comedians make of old people.

Those comedians are so disrespectful.

They don't care whose feelings they hurt.

It gives me satisfaction to realize that one day <u>they</u> will be old.

They will be old, that is, unless they get run over by a truck.

That thought gives me satisfaction as well. (Fun)

I really don't wish them any harm.

Example 22

I wish <u>understanding</u> from them.

I never like it when others' feelings are hurt.

But people get their feelings hurt for a variety of reasons.

Sometimes people get their feelings hurt for <u>no</u> apparent reason.

Controlling the world to prevent hurt feelings isn't possible.

I don't need others to modify their behavior to soothe my feelings.

I can take care of that myself.

I guess I wanted to protect others from having their feelings hurt.

I realize that their feelings are their responsibility.

Comedians have a way of centering on sensitive issues that touch a nerve in the public.

I'm learning that a nerve is always touched in me before I seek vibrational improvement.

I guess I'll start listening for what's funny and stop being so sensitive.

Example 23

My Daughter Lies Constantly

Example: "My daughter will stand before me and tell me an obvious lie without flinching at all. It would be humorous if it didn't make me so angry. She lies about nearly everything. She even lies about insignificant things. I've always believed that honesty is the best policy, and I've never set the example of lying. Why is she doing this? It's very upsetting."

Each of you has come into your physical body understanding that you are a powerful creator, but you are born into an environment that, right from the beginning, demands your compliance. When you are younger, your sense of *who-you-really-are* is stronger, but as those who surround you introduce their interests, ideas, and demands into your experience, you begin to feel the splitting of your own Energies. Usually this integration is gradual enough that those who surround you are satisfied that you are coming along in their intentional socialization process, but sometimes very powerful Beings (like your daughter) rebel.

In the beginning, this rebellion is usually not even pointed at anything specific, and often it is not even conscious on the part of the children. They simply feel intense negative emotions as the influence from others causes a splitting of their own Energy. And, like anyone who wants to feel good but doesn't, they

usually place the blame for their intense discomfort upon whom-
ever they are interacting with at the time they are feeling it. And so,
it is logical that most children would direct most of their negative
emotions due to their disconnection toward their parents, since
their parents are the ones who are most consistently and most significantly attempting to influence them. So, sometimes the lying
is symptomatic of the intense discomfort they are feeling due to
their realization that they are being put in an impossible position
of pleasing everyone.

People often think that children who can be easily guided, who
always do what is asked of them, and who are easily compliant are
very good children. But children who have minds of their own—
who do not want to go along with the ideas of others—are often
regarded as troublesome and difficult. Problems do not usually arise
until their own life experience has caused them to put things in
their own Vibrational Escrow (that they are being called toward)
and then someone else in their life tries to keep them from following that calling. Most of the struggle between parents and children
exists because parents are not willing to allow their children to live
the lives that the children have come forth to live. *Parents are usually extremely well intentioned, wanting what <u>they</u> have been taught to
believe is best for their child, but every person who comes forth into this
physical experience comes with his or her own purpose and plan.*

By laying out guidelines and rules, and by carefully watching
your children to be sure they are doing as you say, you are actually
undermining an essential tenet of their very existence. You are not
allowing *them* to choose. And often you project the attitude that
you do not trust them. And, for most, once they get a whiff of that
from you, you are not then well received, since it is so contrary to
the understanding of their own *Inner Being.* In other words, the less
time they can spend around you and that attitude, the better they
like it.

When anyone gets between you and your intention to be the
creator of your own experience, watch out, because it never works
out well.

*When you present strong rules to your children—or to anyone—you
are, without meaning to, actually cultivating the perfect environment for
lying. When your children observe your positive response when they keep
your rules and your negative response whenever they break your rules,*

Example 23

often your response becomes their dominant intention, and how they achieve that response becomes a lesser issue. They lie to you in an effort to keep you feeling good.

Nothing can fill the void caused by disconnection with your own *Inner Being* other than reconnection with it; and once you have discovered the wonderful experience of managing your own Connection with Source, then you can encourage the same in your children. As your children witness your clarity, lightheartedness, and your overall Well-Being, you will teach them, through the power of your own example, how to connect with their own guidance. And that understanding is much more valuable than getting them to comply with any rules that you might impose.

It is an interesting thing to see. Your daughter, for whatever reason, is not connected to Source, and therefore she feels bad. You observe in her what you do not want to see; therefore, you are not Connected to Source, and so *you* feel bad. You blame your daughter for the way you feel. Your daughter blames you for the way *she* feels, and on it goes.

As you deliberately reach for *downstream* thoughts regarding your daughter (even though your current evidence doesn't easily evoke them), and you manage to release your resistance and come into alignment with *who-you-really-are,* it will become easier and easier for you to see your daughter through the eyes of your Broader Perspective. And as you achieve that, it is our absolute promise that you will inspire the Connection within your daughter, as well.

When you are in alignment with who-you-really-are, *you will only be seeing the very best in your daughter. And when your daughter is in alignment with* who-she-really-is, *she will have no reason to tell you lies.*

There is no greater gift that a parent could give to their children than the example of being aligned with their own guidance. And so, as you become one who consistently looks for and finds *downstream* thoughts of alignment, your children will learn to maintain their Connection with that broader guidance as well—and then this gift of thriving can be passed on from generation to generation.

So begin where you are, and reach for improved feelings about your daughter:

My daughter lies to me when the truth would serve her better.

I don't understand her need to tell me lies.

More often than not, when a person lies, it comes back and bites them.

I don't want my daughter to develop patterns that are bad for her.

I realize that everyone has their own individual point of view.

And while I don't understand her reasons, I can see that she may have some of her own.

I wish she trusted me with the truth.

If my own response to her had always come from my place of Connection, maybe she would now trust me more.

I can't go back and undo anything I've done, but I can begin to be more allowing of her now.

I can see that she sometimes lies in an attempt to be seen in a more positive light.

I also understand that whenever she is lying, she is not in alignment with who-she-really-is.

I want my effort to be about inspiring her alignment, not punishing her for not being in alignment.

I can see how her lie is a manifestation of her lack of Connection, and her lack of Connection is what I want to soothe.

My concern now isn't for the lies themselves, but is instead for the reason for the lies.

I don't want to stop her lies, so much as to enhance her Connection to her Source.

This sweet girl has often been Connected to Source.

When she was little, she was the source of my inspiration on a daily basis.

I have it in me to return the favor.

Example 24

I Keep Getting Passed Over for Promotions at Work

Example: "I've been working for the same company for many years, and I probably know this company better than anyone who works here. In fact, I believe I know it better than the owner of the company! There's a great deal of variety in my work, and I do like that, but it often feels as if things are assigned to me because no one else wants to do them. And since I've been here so long, I can do about everything that needs to be done.

"Last week an employee who hasn't been here half as long as I have was promoted to shop supervisor even though I thought I was next in line and more qualified. I can't understand why that position wasn't offered to me. I feel like quitting."

Every subject is really two subjects: (1) what is wanted, and (2) the lack of what is wanted. Right now you are focused upon lack of the promotion. Most would say, "Yes, but I wasn't focused upon the lack of the promotion until I didn't get it." However, what you are thinking and feeling and what comes to you always match. The more unappreciated you *feel*, the more unappreciated you *are*. People say, "Well, if someone would appreciate me, I would *feel* appreciated." But we want you to understand that you have to feel appreciated *in order* to attract appreciation. Your vibration is your point of attraction, and you have control over your vibration because you have control over the direction of your thoughts.

It is not necessary to trace back through your experience to discover when your first strong feelings of being unappreciated began, for that usually only serves to activate those vibrations in a stronger way and cause you to feel worse. Instead, you can start right where you are and reach for better-feeling thoughts.

People from all walks of life commonly complain that less-deserving people are claiming the rewards that they believe are due *them,* but we want you to understand that no one receives anything unfairly. *The Law of Attraction responds fairly, consistently, and power-fully to the vibrations that you are emitting; and if what is happening in your experience does not please you, you have only to identify what you would prefer, focus upon it until it is easy for you to focus in that way—and then it will be yours.*

Further, if something that you want doesn't come to you and, in fact, you see another win the prize, so to speak, there is even benefit for you in that situation as well, because your Vibrational Escrow just became stronger and clearer, and the forces of the Universe are now flowing more powerfully on your behalf. But as you stand in an attitude of complaint, you are pointed *upstream* while your new-and-improved creation is *downstream.* And so, the more you "want it," the worse you feel.

We want you to realize that you cannot fail, because every moment of your life is causing an evolution of your desires, and the forces of the Universe are working toward their fulfillment. You are the only one who could ever stand in the way and prevent the receiving of those desires. And the good news is, when you are hindering the desires, your negative, *upstream* emotion is letting you know that you are doing so, right now.

An interesting way to approach this situation is this: Look at the person who received the promotion and feel glad that it angered you so, for the strong emotion you are feeling means the creation of an improved working environment is strong within you.

Then feel glad . . .

. . . that you are aware of the anger and hurt feelings, for that means your *Guidance System* is working.

. . . that this uncomfortable situation has been clarifying, and that your Vibrational Escrow is bigger and better than before this all happened.

Example 24

. . . that you have the ability, right now, if you want to, to let go of the oars and begin moving toward your own even more stunning promotion.

. . . that there are no limits to the promotions that are being lined up on your behalf.

. . . that by paying attention to the way you feel and by reaching consistently for the relief of a *downstream* thought, a never-ending stream of wonderful opportunities will come your way.

When you are focused upon your desires and are therefore consistently feeling good because you are in complete alignment, you emit a vibrational résumé—and opportunities appear everywhere before you. *When you've practiced the feeling of success, successful people are drawn to you. When you are practicing the feeling of disappointment, successful people cannot find you. Even if you are standing very near them, they still cannot see you because you are out of alignment with the success they are seeking.*

It is possible for a nearsighted employer to overlook your value and choose someone else, but the Universe at large has you squarely in its sights, and it is not possible for your value to be overlooked. Instead, your precise value is being specifically lined up for the most satisfying rendezvous imaginable.

Do not let some insignificant letdown point you upstream away from all that you desire. Instead, make the best of where you are, reach for better-feeling thoughts, and prepare yourself to be surprised and amazed by the caliber of promotions that are laid out before you on your never-ending journey of expansion.

So begin where you are and try to find improved, *downstream* thoughts:

No matter how long I'm here or how dedicated I am, I'm still overlooked.

I'll never get promoted because I've done everything humanly possible, and still didn't get the promotion.

There are unfair factors at play that I don't understand.

While you may very well be justified in what you are thinking and feeling, these are all *upstream* thoughts of powerlessness. Continue reaching:

That position should have been mine.

I know my employer knows I'm more qualified, so what reason could he possibly have for making this unfair decision?

I should just quit—it would be interesting to watch this guy managing without me.

Then they'll find out who has been holding it all together all this time.

Ah, the sweet relief of revenge! You are still in an extremely negative state of Being, but compared to the powerlessness you have been feeling, this is an improvement. Continue reaching:

I know I'm not the only one who's working hard at work.

There are many people who are deserving of more appreciation and rewards than they are receiving.

It's not my intent to shut the place down, causing hardship for so many.

It's not my intent to quit, causing hardship for my family and myself.

I'm probably not the only one who would have liked this promotion.

I'm probably not the only one who felt deserving of it, either.

I can pull myself together and make the best of this.

I'm going to watch the guy who got the promotion and look for traits that may have made the difference.

I'm willing to learn and expand.

It's possible that this particular promotion wasn't really in my best interests.

There may be something even better for me coming down the road.

When I really think about it, I'm probably not ready for the responsibility of that particular promotion.

I like that it made me think, though.

Example 24

I feel energized from the process.

I can feel how this has expanded my awareness and my horizons.

I'm not unhappy with the way this has unfolded.

I'm actually quite happy with where I am.

I feel eager about what's still to come.

ঌঌঌ ঌঌঌ

Example 25

I Do Not Have the Time or Money to Care for My Parents, and I Feel Guilty

Example: "Both of my parents are sick and can no longer care for themselves. I live hundreds of miles away from them and have a full-time job, so I can't personally take care of them. So, their doctor has advised me to find a place for them where they can be taken care of. They've always worked hard, but they haven't managed to save any money at all, and they have very few assets that could be converted to cash. I've done some checking, and I find that I can't afford the kind of facility I'd like them to be in, and the other options are far less than pleasing. I feel terrible about this."

When we meet parents who are worried about their children, we always tell them that they are not helping the children with their worry; and when we meet children who are worried about their parents, we tell them exactly the same thing: Your concern and worry do not help, but are instead indicators that you are cutting yourself off from help.

Whenever you see what you do not want, like the failing health of someone you love, you send strong vibrational-rocket requests into your own Vibrational Escrow. And so, while you do not realize it right now, for as long as you have known your parents—and especially during those years you have been feeling concern about them—your Vibrational Escrow has expanded substantially on their behalf.

But during your moments of concern and worry, you are so staunchly pointed in opposition to your own desires for your parents that you could not possibly have access to even one good idea that would help them. However, as you learn to ignore the worrisome thoughts and guide yourself more consistently to *downstream* thoughts about this subject, many circumstances and events will unfold offering solutions to your problems and answers to your questions.

You cannot solve the health-care crisis in this world, but that is not your work. Your work is only to come into alignment with your own personal desires—and you have many desires regarding your parents. You will know by the way you are feeling if you are pointing *downstream* toward solutions; and while you may feel good for a while without seeing evidence of improved conditions, it is not possible for you to consistently point *downstream* regarding something that is important to you without beginning to see results. And as you appreciate any evidence of your alignment, more will follow.

Since you are faced with what feels like an immediate crisis, it feels to you that you have no pleasing options whatsoever. As you go over and over this in your mind, considering one unpleasant option after another, your discomfort grows; and from where you stand, feeling as you are feeling, no viable solutions can show themselves to you. In other words, solutions cannot come while the problem rages within you. You must find a way to soothe the feeling of the problem.

You may argue that you would feel soothed if your parents' health would improve, or if they had enough money to pay for their own private care, or if there were a wonderful facility nearby that would give them care at no cost, or if you had enough money that you could hire people to help them . . . but those conditions do not exist, and you have no way of *making* them exist right now. And so, most people, faced with unpleasant situations over which they have no control, just continue to worry—but from that place of worry, you have no access to solutions.

Your only option right now is to find a way of feeling better. And while you may not realize it at first, that is a significant option, for as you are able to feel better, without the unpleasant situation actually changing, your vibration will shift, causing you

Example 25

to come into closer alignment with the clarified desires that you hold regarding your parents. And when you come into alignment with what you want most for them, many doors will begin to open for you, obvious paths will appear before you, and you will know what to do.

Viable solutions to every situation surround you at all times, but in your state of worry or blame or concern (we could insert a very long list of negative emotions here), you cannot see those solutions.

So make an effort to improve the way you feel. Remember, your objective here is not to actually find the solution at this time, but only to find relief. In fact, when you are determined to find a solution before you have lined up your energy, you nearly always turn *upstream* instead of *downstream*. Relief is your goal here:

I'm so worried about my parents.

I don't know what will happen to them.

I wish they'd taken better care of themselves.

I wish they'd made better financial plans for their future.

Those statements accurately reflect where you are. Now reach for thoughts that give you relief:

No decision needs to be made today.

Although this has been building, there's plenty of time to figure it out.

I know how it is that in one moment there are no good ideas, and in the next, there is a good idea.

Before an answer comes, it often feels like it will never come; and then when the answer does arrive, you wonder why you ever doubted that it was coming.

Now already you are feeling better, and even with this short time of self-soothing, ideas may begin to flow to you. It is our encouragement, however, that you resist the temptation to jump into action too soon, because the better you feel before you jump into action, the more appropriate the action will be and the more positive the outcome you will receive.

There must be many others who find themselves in similar circumstances.

I'm certain that many people find themselves in this situation.

That means that many people have been asking for solutions.

And when people ask, the answers are always given, so there are certainly many viable solutions waiting to be discovered.

We may very well allow our own unique solution.

It will be so satisfying once I make that discovery.

As things shift in me to allow my access to wonderful solutions, perhaps things are shifting in our culture, at large, to allow more widespread solutions.

What others are allowing—or not—does not affect me.

I'm eagerly awaiting an easy flow of good ideas to facilitate my parents' care.

When you realize that a brief exercise like this is all that you need to do at this time, you are on your way. Not only is it all that you *need* to do, it is all that you *can* do—but it is enough. When you feel better, you have released resistance; and in the absence of resistance, a clear path lights up before you, which leads you, step-by-step, to the solutions you seek.

ঙ্গ ঙ্গ ঙ্গ ঞ্চ ঞ্চ ঞ্চ

Example 26

I Am Wasting My Life Stuck in Traffic

Example: "I live in a big city with millions of people, and the traffic is terrible. I commute over an hour each way to and from my place of employment, and that's when things are going well. But there are times when I'm stuck in traffic for hours because of road construction or an accident.

"I guess I could try to find a home that's closer to my work, but there are so many things for me to consider. It isn't easy to find everything my family and I want in a house that at the same time is near enough to my work to make that much difference. But I feel like I'm wasting my life sitting in traffic."

No matter what it is that people desire, one of the greatest hindrances that slows the process of receiving it—and sometimes keeps them from ever obtaining it—is their fixation upon where they stand in relationship to where they want to be.

People will say, "I want to be over *there*, but here I am, over *here*." And since *here*, where they stand, is so easy for them to observe, it usually dominates the bulk of the vibrations that they offer. You may be thinking, *Yes, but this is a situation where I really __am__ here, and I would really rather be there—and I can't physically pick myself up and transport myself to another location.* But we want you to understand that whether you want to be well from your place of sickness, or slender from your place of fatness, or rich from your place of poverty, or flowing in traffic rather than stuck in traffic, the dynamics of creation are the same: When you want something and you believe that having it will make you feel good; if, right now, you feel bad, you are not moving toward what you want. . . . *You have to feel good now, no matter what the conditions are, or the conditions cannot improve. You must make peace, so to speak, with where you are to allow yourself to move to a place you would rather be.*

People often worry that making peace with an unpleasant situation is equivalent to giving in and accepting it, so that now the unwanted will only remain longer . . . but that is not what happens at all. When you make peace with where you are, you feel better—or turn *downstream,* so to speak—and flow toward what you do want. Whenever you writhe in discomfort or whine and complain, you are turned *upstream* and away from what you want for the duration of your discomfort.

The more you complain about traffic, the more you prevent improvement in your situation. Some would say that traffic is what it is, so your experience within it is not in your control—but there is nothing that affects you over which you have no control. However, you cannot effect positive change from your position of lack. *Any action that is taken from a place of negative emotion will not yield positive results.*

If you are able to bring yourself from a position of discomfort into a peaceful position of feeling good even though no outside condition has changed, in a short time the outside condition *must* change. If you continue to observe an unpleasant condition, making no effort to find a better-feeling way of seeing it, the condition will not only *not* improve, but the *Law of Attraction* will bring further evidence to support it. The things you are observing cannot change until you see them in a different way. Many people say, "Give me more money and then I'll feel more prosperous." We say, "You must feel more prosperous and then more money will come."

The key to Deliberate Creation is simply to decide how you want to feel and then to figure out a way to feel that way, now. And when you do, everything around you will acquiesce to your newfound basis of attraction—the powerful Law of Attraction is utterly cooperative and absolutely precise.

Example 26

A clear route or path from where you are to where you want to be is always available, but when you are feeling negative emotion, you cannot find it. As you consistently feel good, your timing will improve, new ideas will occur to you; road improvements that have been bogged down in committees will be freed up, work projects you have wanted will show up around the corner, your employer will tell you that he wants you to work from home. . . . The resources of the Universe are vast and unlimited—and now you have access to them.

So begin where you are and reach for improved-feeling thoughts.

> *Why would I choose to live in a place where I spend all of my time sitting here breathing in fumes?*
>
> *I can hardly bear to sit here—I want to abandon my car and just run off into the bushes.*

We have offered this exaggerated example of how some feel as they are stuck in traffic in order to amplify something significant: The way you are feeling right now as you are stuck in traffic is rarely only *because* you are right now stuck in traffic. In other words, those who are pleased with how life is going, happy in their relationships, thriving financially, feeling good in their bodies, are not nearly as bothered about being stuck in traffic as others who are out there hanging on the raw-and-ragged edge of life regarding other aspects of their life experience.

However, no matter how you feel or how bad it is, and no matter what the reasons are why you feel so bad, your work is still exactly the same: *From where you are, make an effort to feel just a little bit of relief.*

If your discomfort as you are stuck in traffic is really only a feeling of frustration *because* you are stuck in traffic, you will be able to easily bring yourself to a better-feeling place. And as you do so consistently, day after day, while you are sitting in slow-moving traffic, you will begin to receive impulses that will serve you. Your timing as you enter the roadways will improve. Your impulse to exit the freeway and take the surface roads for a distance will serve you. In your state of alignment, you will begin to move with other drivers in a sort of cosmic dance that you will find amazing and exhilarating. The entire Universe cooperates with you when you are in the flow of your own Vibrational Stream.

I think that I'll use this time to ponder some important things.

Since thinking is more important than action, I'll use this time of not much action to think.

It's fun to observe other people in the cars around me.

It's sort of like going to a party where you can see other people in other conversations even though you are not personally conversing with them.

It's fun to guess what they're discussing or what their life is about.

I enjoy the wide variety of people, vehicles, and stories that surround me in traffic.

I like the idea of using my own thoughts to create my own story.

I like the idea of my story radiating out of me and out of my vehicle.

It's fun to get tuned in to my best-feeling self and then notice the other drivers that notice me.

It may very well turn out that my favorite part of life is slowly moving down this freeway, watching the evidence of my own vibrational offering.

(Here's a new dilemma for future discussion: "I sometimes miss the slow-moving traffi during which I did my very best thinking.")

ॐ ॐ ॐ ॐ ॐ ॐ

Example 27

Now That I Know about the *Law of Attraction*, My Thoughts Worry Me

Example: "I'm having a hard time controlling my thoughts, and that really worries me now that I know that I'm attracting to me the essence of whatever it is that I'm thinking about. I think I was happier before I knew about the *Law of Attraction*, because now my thoughts scare me. Sometimes I find myself thinking about something really awful, and then I worry that just because I was thinking about it, it's going to happen."

It is very good when you are aware that your thoughts are scaring you because it means that you can feel the results of your own <u>Guidance System.</u> In other words, when you feel fear, it means that your in-this-moment thought is contrary to the thoughts your *Inner Being* is having about this subject. So when you think about bad things happening, it is logical that your *Inner Being* would not join you in those kinds of thoughts.

The very emotion of fear that you are describing is only your *Guidance System* letting you know that you are thinking an *upstream* thought of resistance. Fear does not mean that something bad is going to happen immediately. But it does mean that this is an *upstream* thought.

If you remain pointed *upstream* long enough, you could deprive yourself of the Well-Being that is natural. But it need not take you long to get into the habit of thinking *downstream* thoughts. *With a little bit of practice, you will discover how easy it is to let go of those oars of resistance—and when you consistently release your feelings of fear by deliberately directing your thoughts, it will not be possible for bad things to occur in your experience.*

As you are consistently feeling good and flowing toward the things you desire, those close to you will be influenced by your example, until it is possible that you could positively influence your children, your mate, your parents, your siblings, and your friends to more positive Deliberate Creation. . . . We do not want you to be afraid of fear. We *do* want you to understand it and benefit by the guidance that it offers you. Fear simply means you are pointed *upstream,* and we want you to understand that you have to point *upstream* for a significant time with great consistency before you disallow your Well-Being to the point of a truly negative creation. And even if a negative thing does occur, you have the ability to regroup, get refocused, and create differently the next time.

Many people would explain that their fear was natural and assert that it was valid, as they point out the bad things that are happening in their lives or in the lives of others they care about, but the reason why people sometimes go from one negative experience to another is simply because when the first unwanted thing happens, they give a great deal of their attention to it, which then creates the second . . . and so on. Most people do offer the majority of their thoughts in response to the things in their life that they are observing. Some stubbornly ask, "But how did the first negative thing come about?" And our answer is: *Everything that happens to you is but a by-product of your consistent thoughts and feelings.*

Others often argue, "But what about the little children? How is it that they would create something so negative in their experience?" We want you to understand that even though a little child may not be speaking in words, at no time is that child not emitting a vibration that the *Law of Attraction* is responding to.

All of you learn to offer your vibrations from the environment that surrounds you. Even while in your mother's womb, you were picking up vibrations from her and from her surroundings. But there is no reason to be unhappy about anything that has affected you previously, for you have complete power, right here and now, to choose improved-feeling thoughts. And now that you understand

Example 27

the Stream of Life, and that you can always tell by the way you feel whether you are pointed *downstream* toward the fulfillment of your desires or *upstream* in resistance to your desires, you will never again be negatively influenced without your knowledge.

All of you understood, when you made the decision to come forth into this body, that you would be surrounded by a smorgasbord of thoughts, and that some of them would be to your liking and some would not. But not one of you wished for a limiting of the environment into which you were being born, for you understood then—as you are coming to remember now—the power of your own *Guidance System* and the value of the diversity from which you would make your choices.

With a little practice, you will not only no longer fear your thoughts, but you will take delight in them . . . for there is not a more delicious moment than one in which you have directed your thoughts to harmonize with the Broader Perspective of your Being. When you observe the people, places, and experiences of your world through the eyes of your *Inner Being,* they do not frighten you—they delight you!

So, begin where you are and reach for the relief of the better-feeling thoughts:

I'm not good at controlling my thoughts.

I catch myself in the middle of unpleasant thoughts all day long.

At times, though, I do contemplate very positive things.

I've noticed that positive topics expand in my mind, also.

I do see that the <u>Law of Attraction</u> is giving me more thoughts that are like my current active thought.

I could choose more deliberately which thought I decide to make the active thought.

I do know that when I know what I <u>don't</u> want, I also know what I <u>do</u> want.

I could lean more deliberately in a more positive direction.

There are many positive things happening in my life.

I do know that there's more going on that's positive than negative.

This must mean my thoughts are leaning more in the positive direction.

It's not necessary for every thought I think to be a perfectly positive thought.

It isn't even possible to think only positive thoughts.

My work is merely to lean in a positive direction.

I think I'm doing that.

I'm doing that much more so now than a few weeks ago.

I'm directing my thoughts.

Not only do I <u>feel</u> better these days, but <u>things are turning out better for me</u>.

I now see that the evidence I'm looking for is an improved feeling rather than a changed condition.

I also know that a consistently improved feeling will be the forerunner of an improved condition.

I not only understand the process of creation—I am effectively applying it.

Example 28

My Husband Is Very Sick

Example: "The doctors are telling us that my husband is very sick, and they aren't suggesting any more treatment because they don't believe that there are any more medical alternatives. He's been dealing with this illness for a few years now, and I guess that as long as the doctors were still making suggestions, we believed he would eventually recover. But now we're both feeling hopeless and frightened.

"I don't know what to do, and I don't know what I should be saying to him. Should I continue to hold out hope for his recovery, or should I be preparing him—and myself—for his death?"

It is not easy to find your own balance when you are watching someone you care about experiencing the physical and mental discomfort of an illness. Even though you have lived with this man for many years and your lives are intertwined in so many ways, you have no way of really understanding his mix of vibrations between his day-to-day thoughts and the vibrations of his *Inner Being.* Only your own mix of vibrations is truly available to you.

Family members often have such a strong opinion of what *they* desire regarding the illness of their loved one that they hinder more than they help, but it is possible, even under these intense conditions, to find and maintain *your* balance. And when you do, you help—every time.

You cannot think for your husband, and you cannot create his reality . . . but you can think for yourself, and you can create your own reality. And when you find your own true alignment, your power of influence is very strong.

So, some might say, "Then I will find my alignment—whatever that takes—and then I will influence my mate to his recovery." But *we* would say, instead: "I will find my alignment and therefore influence him to *his* alignment, and then he can do as *he* truly desires to do." And there are big differences in those two statements.

Sickness is always due to a vibrational imbalance. In every case, sickness means that an individual has a strong Current flowing, but he or she is pointed *upstream* for some reason. As they ponder the problems of the world in which they live, most people think thoughts that cause internal resistance because often they are unaware of the vibrations within them. Even babies are influenced by these *upstream* vibrations as they acclimate to the environment that surrounds them.

Scientists and doctors continually seek cures for the illnesses of their times, and so they offer a never-ending stream of changing options in medicine, treatment, and diet. But they will continue to lose more ground each year as more diseases are discovered than are cured, until they come to the following understanding: *Rather than seeking a medical cure for a disease, you must understand the vibrational cause of it, for there is not enough action in the world to compensate for misaligned Energy.*

So there is great reason for you to feel hopeful again about your husband's recovery, for now that the medical community has given up on him, he is now more likely to turn his attention to the only thing that really ever works anyway: the alignment of his own Being. It is not uncommon for humans to wait until they have run out of action alternatives before they make an effort at aligning their own Energy. And then, when the recovery comes, the doctors pronounce it to be a miracle, but it is not a miracle at all—it is simply a realigning of thoughts, vibrations, and Energy.

Since whenever you know what you *do not* want, you always know more clearly what you *do* want, your husband has been adding to his Vibrational Escrow relative to his physical body in

Example 28

a powerful way for a while now—which means that his Stream is moving very fast. In other words, the sicker people are, the more rockets of desire for wellness they are sending into their Vibrational Escrow, but as that Stream moves faster and their *Inner Being* calls them even more powerfully toward the expansion of wellness, if they don't turn and go in the direction of the wellness, then they become sicker still.

You see how it works? So you could accurately say, "The sicker I am, the more potential for wellness I have set into motion. . . ." It is actually easier to recover from something deadly than it is to get over something minor—because the deadly thing has put so much power in Vibrational Escrow. Your willingness to feel good is the only requirement.

Since your husband is the only one who has vibrational control of his Being, you cannot do this work for him. It is *your* work to maintain your own vibrational balance, even in the midst of this unsettling situation; and as you are able to do that, your power of influence will be very strong. Under these circumstances, you may easily find unsettling thoughts, but you must guide your mind to better-feeling thoughts—not for your husband's sake, but for your own. And then, when you are in alignment with your desire, you will have a positive influence on him.

If you seek your own alignment, apart from wanting to help your husband, it will be much more possible for you to help him. But if you seek alignment so that you can help him, you will more likely be focused upon his illness—therefore, you will not find your alignment; and so, you will not be offering the powerful, influential vibration that is possible when you are in alignment.

Nearly everyone you would meet would tell you that the way you feel is really dependent upon your husband's improvement, but we want you to understand that you must find a way to feel good whether he gets better or worse, or lives or dies . . . for only when you are selfish enough to do that can you help him.

Try to find some better-feeling thoughts, beginning where you are:

I want to help my husband get well.

The doctors say that there's no hope.

I can't find my place, because I don't want to give up, but I feel foolish holding out hope.

I've gone from being terrified at the idea of him dying to being resigned that he's going to die.

And I feel guilty about giving in to the idea of him dying.

I feel that I should be the last one to give in.

Feel the futility in trying to sort this out. Now turn your attention to something you can control. Try to improve the way you feel. Do not try to save your husband's life. Do not try to sort out the issues of life and death. Do not try to reform the doctors or make medicine better. Do the only thing that you can do: Improve the way you feel by deliberately choosing your thoughts.

Some days I feel unbearable emotional discomfort, and some days I feel somewhat better.

I do understand that my emotions, even in these extreme conditions, do vary.

The idea of feeling relief from these debilitating emotions does sound nice.

It does give me comfort to realize that it's not my job to change my husband's condition.

This is helping me realize that there must be huge value in getting a handle on this death thing.

It seems utterly illogical to me that "death," which happens to every single person who has ever lived on this earth or ever will live on this earth, is bad in some way.

I don't want my husband to die, but I do feel relief when I realize that it's not my job to change that.

It feels good to expect to someday completely understand how our physical world meshes with the Non-Physical world.

It does feel good to remember we are all Eternal Beings.

I feel relief in understanding that the "death" experience isn't one of separation.

I'm so glad to know that our thoughts transcend the "death" experience.

Example 28

I like remembering that our relationships are Eternal.

I want my husband to find relief whether he finds it and remains here or releases into his Non-Physical perspective.

It's comforting to me to focus upon his finding relief.

While we would not ask you to come to a complete under-standing and resolution of the "death" subject (which has plagued humankind for such a long time) in one short looking-for-*down-stream*-thoughts effort, we will tell you that your vibration has substantially shifted here. And that is worth much more than most realize. Words do not teach, but life experience does; and as you find the true relief that is only possible by your deliberate directing of your own thoughts, you will radiate a different vibration that can influence the vibration of your husband. And with his desire peaked at this highest-ever level due to the intensity of what he is living, then a little bit of allowing—as you and he both release resistance—can go a very long way.

FROM YOUR PERSPECTIVE, THE BEST THING THAT COULD HAPPEN IS:

- You feel so much better.

- You help him feel so much better.

- His Energies are greatly improved.

- His health returns.

THE WORST THING THAT COULD HAPPEN IS:

- You feel so much better.

- You feel so much better.

- You feel so much better.

- He makes his reemergence into Pure, Positive Energy.

- *He* feels SO MUCH BETTER!

You will never know the wonderful power of your influence toward the Well-Being of all until you come into full alignment with *who-you-really-are.*

৩৫ ৩৫ ৩৫ ৳৯ ৳৯ ৳৯

Example 29

My Lover Left Me

Example: "My boyfriend, whom I've been living with for the last two years, moved out. We didn't agree on everything, and we did fight about some things, but nothing very serious. I thought that we were doing okay, and I can't believe that he doesn't want us to be together anymore. He swears that he's not going to be with someone else, but how can you supposedly love someone and then just all of a sudden move out for no reason?"

Most people who want a relationship believe that a mediocre relationship is better than no relationship at all, but we do not agree with that. In other words, since the potential for a glorious relationship always exists—we never encourage settling for less.

Remember that you feel the way you do because of the mix of vibrations within you, and that no two people feel exactly the same way about anything. It is possible for two people to be sharing what appears to be an identical experience, but one person is enjoying it while the other is not because their individual mixture of vibrations varies.

Rather than trying to figure out what another person wants and then putting your efforts toward satisfying his or her desires, it is much more productive and satisfying for you to be directing your thoughts toward the things that *you* desire.

Whatever you are living is causing you to make regular deposits into your Vibrational Escrow account, so anytime something happens that you do not want, you send out a request for what you prefer instead. So, for example, now that your lover has left your experience, your request for someone who wants to be with you has been submitted in a stronger, clearer way than ever before.

Many of your experiences throughout this lifetime have caused you to make requests, and so you have created a magnificent relationship that waits for you in Vibrational Escrow and calls you toward the fulfillment of it. And as you find more *downstream* thoughts, you get closer to the realization of these desires. But today, while your heart is breaking, you are going against the Current, and you are not allowing yourself to get closer to the relationship that waits for you.

People are often amazed when we tell them that every bad thing that has ever happened to them in a relationship is part of the reason why such a magnificent relationship now waits for them. However, if they continue to beat the drum of those bad things that have happened, they will continue to deprive themselves of the discovery of that wonderful creation.

Some might argue that even though it seems that someone abruptly made a decision and left, there had to be signs of your relationship breaking down that you were missing, and that if you had been more tuned in to your boyfriend, you might have been able to turn this around—if you had caught the trouble at an earlier stage. But we are quite pleased that you did not see this coming, because that means you were not looking for trouble. And we can also tell that you were predominantly focused upon the positive aspects of your relationship.

Question: "So, if I was predominantly thinking positive thoughts, then why did he leave me?"

This is something that we really want you to come to understand: When you are predominantly feeling good, all things are aligning for your ultimate satisfaction. In other words, your life, with its ups and downs, has caused you to create a Vibrational Escrow of a wonderful future life experience, and you are being called toward it. So whenever you are feeling good, that wonderful

Example 29

future is in the process of making its way to you and you to it. *Simply put, anyone who moves out of your experience, for any reason, was not a match to the wonderful future that is waiting for you in Vibrational Escrow.*

Here is something else that you may find fascinating: Let us say that you were watching your boyfriend closely in your desire to please him in every way possible, and you had begun to notice that he was beginning to be unhappy and no longer completely satisfied in your relationship. And then, in your awareness of his unhappiness, you began to feel worried, and so you tried harder and harder to make him happy. The most important thing that we want you to understand is that in your focus, which caused your unhappiness, you are no longer a match to your own desires. So you are now moving *upstream,* not *downstream.* . . . You are a match to his unhappiness, not to your true desires; and in that situation, you would probably hold him in your experience longer. In other words, by focusing upon your boyfriend's unhappiness—and in your efforts to modify conditions to bring him to a happier place—you are actually becoming more out of alignment with *who-you-really-are* and what you really want. You have soothed him, and so he stays longer . . . and many think that is success. But from the bigger picture, what has happened is that you have worked to please *him* instead of yourself. And under those conditions, in time *you* would be the one who would be wanting to leave.

By being unaware of his discomfort, and by continuing to focus upon positive aspects in your relationship, you remained true to your real vision of a relationship—and since he is not matching that true vision, he is leaving. And, friend, we promise you, that is not a bad thing. . . . *When you consistently feel good, even when people are freaking out around you—and even leaving you—what you really want must find you. It will be more difficult now, but in the same way you did not let his increasing unhappiness affect you, if you can now not allow his leaving to upset you, then the relationship that you have been crafting all along will come to you. And then your work will be the same again: to look for positive aspects. Do not get drawn into anyone's drama.* <u>*Do not stand on your head to please others in a distorted way of soothing their misalignment. It is better to let those things that are not a match leave your experience.*</u>

This pain you are feeling is multifaceted, as it touches on so many things that matter to you. Not only do you feel unloved when what you want is love, but you feel insecure when what you want is security; you feel abandoned while what you want is to be adored. And while we understand that so soon after your lover has left you, it is not easy to find good-feeling thoughts, still, that must be your dominant intention.

The Law of Attraction *is matching you up with circumstances, events, and other people who match your vibration. And so, if you will deliberately choose your vibration—especially one that matches your own specifically created Vibrational Escrow—someone you would consider to be a perfect mate must come to you.* Conversely, if you do not line up with the lover you really want, you will attract a lover who matches how you *feel;* and if you *feel* abandoned, you can only attract another who will behave in the same way.

With far less time and effort than you think, you can come into alignment with your idea of a perfect relationship; and there will be a time, not so far from now, when you will look back on this lover who just left you with great appreciation for the serious contribution he helped you make toward the creation of your perfect mate. You may want to write him a letter that says:

> *Thank you for breaking my heart and, in the process, helping me to clarify what I really want. Thank you for the painful experience of giving birth to such powerful rockets of desire that when I turned in the direction of that desire, I was swiftly transported into this blissful relationship. It is my desire that your interaction with me has provided you with the same wonderful benefit.*

Many people work very hard to try to make things work out. But we want you to understand that when you work to bring yourself into alignment with You—rather than into alignment with what someone else wants you to be—then the Universe will bring you the match. Just work to maintain your alignment, and the Universe will deliver to you partners who are aligned. It is *Law*.

So start where you are and reach for increasingly better-feeling thoughts:

Example 29

I'm in a state of shock and depression; I don't know what to do.

I can't believe this has happened—I thought he was the one.

Why would he lead me on like that?

Why would he pretend that he wanted to be with me forever?

Now, see if you can move from your feeling of powerlessness. Reach for something that makes you at least feel like getting out of bed:

This is the last time something like this will happen to me.

I don't deserve to be treated like this.

I'm glad that he left, because clearly he's not who I thought he was.

Negative as these thoughts are, they are giving you a feeling of relief. Keep going:

Clearly we aren't right for each other.

There's no point in wasting more time figuring that out.

This was an extremely clarifying situation for me.

I've learned so much in such a short period of time.

Thinking back, I could sort of feel this coming.

At the time, I didn't want to see it, but now I realize it had been coming.

I'm not sorry that this has happened.

Nothing terrible has really happened here.

It's not a bad thing to find out that what I really want is somewhere else.

This relationship has helped me to more clearly define who I am and what I'm looking for.

I feel newly energized regarding relationships.

I'm going to take my time as I move forward.

There's no urgency about figuring this out.

I'm actually happy to have some breathing space.

In a strange way, I'm looking forward to what comes next.

I know that what will come next will be better because of this relationship.

Someday I may thank him for helping me to get clear about what I do want.

However, that day is not today.

Well, maybe it is—a little.

You have to admit you do feel better. And *that* is your only work. If you will continue to feel good, everything that you desire must come!

ᵉᵍᵉᵍᵉᵍ ᵇᵃᵇᵃᵇᵃ

Example 30

My Pet Is Sick

Example: "My dog is relatively young, but he's sick all the time. My veterinarian bills are enormous because it seems that as soon as my dog gets over one thing, then he gets sick with something else. I love my dog, and I don't want him to suffer or to die, but I also don't want to have to keep taking him to the vet. What's going on with him?"

Your dog, as with all of the beasts on your planet, is usually much more in alignment with his *Inner Being* than most humans, but the beasts in the wild are more often in alignment than those who spend more time around humans, because the domesticated animals, simply by observing their human co-creators, often begin to split their Energy in the way that humans do. Also, since everyone—human and beast alike—inherently wants freedom, an animal who is confined often feels more resistance than one who is free to roam. It is hard for a human to understand this, but the beasts of your planet would choose freedom over security every time.

Nevertheless, many animals are perfectly happy sharing their environment with humans, and what may appear to you to be an environment of confinement causes no resistance in their overall vibrational alignment. However, your animals never fare well in environments of strong negative emotion. Pure, Positive Energy animals in the wild will run from a human who approaches, not because they fear you, but because you do not feel good to them.

Over time, your domesticated animals begin to adjust to the vibration of humans and are able, for the most part, to maintain their alignment even while interacting with you. And, like you, whatever they give their attention to makes up the vibrational balance of their Being. As they hold you as their object of attention and you are not in alignment with your own Source Energy, they are influenced to less Connection as well. Your animals are resilient, however, and they can easily come back into alignment, for they do not hold grudges and play past scenarios over again in their minds as humans do. Once an uncomfortable situation passes, they let it go—completely.

However, if animals are subjected to daily stress or anger or are made to feel like they are in the way or unwanted, their Energy can get out of balance enough that their bodies will begin to demonstrate evidence of their misalignment.

There are many students of *Deliberate Creation* who really want to understand how to create their own reality, who are working to understand their *Emotional Guidance System,* who want to more consistently fl w *downstream,* and who do not really decide to apply what they know until they discover that they are negatively affecting their pets. It is a bit funny that people will put up with the discomfort of their own negative emotions if the results of that are only impacting them, but when they discover that they are also impacting the lives of their dear pets, then they are willing to try to makes changes.

While it is nice that you care about the Well-Being of your animal, we want you to care about your own Well-Being as well.

If you are pointed *upstream* (feeling negative emotion) and you make no effort to let go of the oars, the *Law of Attraction* will continue to respond to your vibration, your situation will intensify—and you will feel worse.

If you continue to make no effort to release the resistance, the *Law of Attraction* will continue to respond to your vibration, your situation will increase—and you will feel worse still.

If you still continue to make no effort, in time your own physical body will begin to show symptoms of the imbalance.

Example 30

Sometimes your dear pet demonstrates the physical symptoms as a part of your *Guidance System*. It is as if he understands that you are willing to endure negative emotions while you are not willing to negatively influence your pet. And so, often your pet is fulfilling an intention that the two of you set forth before either of you were born into your physical bodies—that of reminding you of your vibrational countenance.

Your pet would also like to help you to get over this "death" thing, for it understands that there is no death, but only Eternal Life. *Your pet joyously romps into physical body after physical body, dreading death never, enjoying its own joyful ride on its own joyful river. Your dog is among the best teachers on the planet.*

So reach for some better-feeling thoughts about your beloved pet:

I wish I understood why my dog continually gets sick.

I can find no value in this at all.

I hate to see him feeling bad, and it's costing me a fortune.

I'm tempted to just let him find his own way, but I don't want him to suffer or die.

I can't afford these veterinarian bills.

Taking him to the veternarian feels bad.

Not taking him feels worse.

Since I can't find an action that gives me relief, maybe I should just try to feel better.

It's possible that this great dog is trying to tell me something.

I'm going to try to stand back from this situation and look for what I can see in it.

One thing I notice right away is that even though my dog clearly doesn't feel well physically, he doesn't seem to be worried about it.

And while he's not frisky like he used to be, his attitude seems mostly positive.

When I speak to him, he always makes an effort to wag his tail a bit.

Sometimes it feels like he's trying to soothe me because I'm worried about him.

I would like to soothe <u>him</u> by not seeming worried about him.

I'm going to make an effort to be more positive about his condition.

I'm going to speak to him in more optimistic terms.

I'll no longer complain about the cost of the veterinarian.

When I'm not with him, I'm going to pretend he has improved.

When I come home from work, I'll look for improvement.

When I see the slightest symptom of him feeling better, I'll talk about that.

I'm going to look for reasons to feel good about him and ignore anything else.

I sense that he's helping me to focus my thoughts deliberately.

I can see how he's a great teacher of unconditional love, as he won't modify this condition so that I can feel better.

I feel that's his message to me: "Feel better because you choose to, not because I'm giving you the reason to feel better."

That's so empowering.

What a great dog!

⊰⊰⊰ ⊱⊱⊱

Example 31

I Have Never Had Enough Money

Example: "I can't remember a time when I wasn't worried about money. Every time I turn around, there's another unexpected expense, and it seems like the things that I need to buy for my family and for myself keep going up and up in price, but my wages aren't going up nearly as fast as my expenses.

"I used to work 40 hours per week, and my wife didn't work outside of our home. Now she has a full-time job, and I work 60 hours per week—and we still never have any extra money. I see other people taking vacations and buying new houses and new cars, and I wonder how they're doing it. What am I missing?"

While it seems logical that your financial budget is only about the simple economics of finding a balance between the money that is coming in and the money that is going out, there is another powerful factor that most people do not understand: You simply cannot offer enough action to compensate for the contradictory Energy of your Being. As you feel the way you do about money, even though your experience certainly justifies the way you feel, things cannot improve because <u>the Law of Attraction is responding to your vibration—not to your actions.</u>

Of course, there are obvious variables in the productivity of *action* that are easy to see: A strong man can pick up a heavier object than a weak man, someone who moves quickly can move more things around in a day than a slow-moving person, a person who types 60 words per minute can accomplish more typing in a day than a person who types 20 words per minute . . . but these variations on *action* are minuscule in comparison with the leverage that you can achieve by aligning your own Energies. In blunt terms, it is not possible to offer enough action to compensate for misaligned Energies.

When you develop *upstream* thought patterns about the lack of money, you prevent your own discovery of avenues that would provide more of it. As you feel frustrated about not having enough money, and you make no effort to find a better-feeling thought about it, your frustration will turn to anger and eventually to fear as your patterns of thought hold you in more consistent *upstream* resistance to your financial Stream of Well-Being. And the worse you feel, the worse it gets—because the worse you feel, the more resistance you are offering that is preventing you from the discovery of the solutions that you are seeking.

In any moment that you are focused upon not having enough money, you are vibrationally asking for more, which makes your Stream move faster. But as you are focused upon not having enough money, you are focused *upstream* while your *Inner Being* is calling you *downstream*. Strong negative emotion about your financial situation is the indication of two significant things:

1. You have requested a great deal of financial assistance that your *Inner Being* is calling you toward.

2. You are pointed *upstream,* in opposition to the money you want.

No matter how many hours you and your wife may work, and no matter how much money flows into your household, you cannot achieve a *financial* balance until you first achieve a *vibrational* balance in your own Being. And in the moment that you let go of the oars and allow yourself to turn in the Stream, you will feel relief in your own body, and the financial relief will come close behind.

When you have wanted something for a long time and have therefore amassed a considerable Vibrational Escrow on the subject, a little bit of relief goes a long way. In other words, if you can

Example 31

manage to get yourself feeling better for a few days, evidence of your releasing of resistance will begin to appear in some form of financial relief.

Now that you understand that you control how much money is flowing, as well as how much of it you let into your experience right now, you may recognize some of the patterns from your own experience that validate this understanding: *The key to consistently getting the good results that you desire is to manage to feel good even when dollars are in short supply. When you learn to manage the way you feel, you will discover the powerful leverage of Energy alignment, and you will see the <u>Law of Attraction</u> deliver veritable fortunes to your door. But if you merely have emotional knee-jerk responses to the conditions you are observing, you will be limited to the paltry amount of money that your physical action yields.*

From wherever you are, start reaching for some better-feeling thoughts:

I'm so tired of not having enough money.

I see no way of <u>ever</u> having enough money.

I work such long hours that I'm tired all the time.

I'm tired of making our budget work by cutting back on thing after thing.

This is how you *feel,* and this is temporarily where you are, but from these kinds of thoughts, money cannot begin to flow into your experience in a more powerful way. You have to change your thoughts and feelings first. However, we are not guiding you to improved thoughts and feelings in order to affect your financial situation. Rather, we are guiding you to improved thoughts and feelings for the sake of the improved vibrational offering. If you will let the improvement in the way you *feel* be your objective, the greater amounts of money must begin to flow to you as you accomplish a consistent improvement in the way you feel.

I work longer hours than any of our neighbors.

Money just seems to come more easily to them.

It seems as if every day someone I know is showing off their new car.

Comparing your condition to that of another will keep you chronically out of balance and confused about the improved direction of your thoughts. However, comparing one of your own thoughts to another of your own thoughts with the singular intention of finding a better-feeling thought will, in a rather short time, give you a clear sense of *downstream* direction.

We aren't doing badly.

We actually do live very well.

My wife and I do have a sense of pride about the things we've accomplished.

We've made good decisions.

We have quite a bit of equity in our home.

If I look at the overall picture, I realize it has been steadily improving.

When I look how far we've come, I see tremendous improvement.

You are feeling so much better already. Now see how much further you can go:

I'll figure this out.

I'm actually quite good at figuring things out.

I'm standing by for inspiration.

Meanwhile, we're doing all right.

It's actually quite pleasant to anticipate expansion.

Sometimes I get a sense of a very bright future.

We have so much life and opportunity ahead of us.

It will be fun to watch this all play out.

Someone watching you in this process would have no way of understanding the powerful work you have done here, because more money has not actually dropped into your lap yet. But when you understand the power of the Stream, and you recognize, by

Example 31

the improvement in the way you feel, the tremendous reduction of resistance that you have just accomplished, you may understand the enormous productivity of this process. And unlike those skeptics who may doubt the power of thought, you are going to have the wonderful firsthand experience of watching things line up around you to accommodate your desires. Others may very well call you "lucky," but you'll know how it happened, because you did it deliberately.

એક એક એક ફેન ફેન ફેન

Example 32

My Dog Died and I Feel Grief

Example: "My dog died, and I feel so bad about it. I knew he wouldn't live forever, and I knew I'd outlive him, but I'm so sad about him being gone. I hate to go home, because every time I walk up to the door I feel sad whenever I remember he won't be there to greet me. Something or other reminds me of him several times every day, and I feel that deep grief all over again. I don't think I should feel this bad about this for this long, but I can't seem to get over it. My friends tell me I should get another dog, but I just can't bring myself to do that. Anyway, wouldn't I just be setting myself up for more pain later?"

People often feel more sadness over the loss of their pet than nearly anything else that they ever experience. Some think this pain is illogical and ill placed, for there are so many other important aspects to life that must surely be more important than your pet. "He suffered more over the death of his dog than when his own dear father died," they have said.

The more you want something, the more you suffer when you focus upon the absence of it. But the pain you are feeling over the death of your dog is not because of the absence of your dog—it is much bigger than that.

Your dog represented Pure, Positive Energy to you. Your dog

remained, throughout his entire life, as you were when you were first born: an extension of Pure, Positive Energy. And often, through your attention to your dog and your interaction with your dog, you were inspired more to your own Connection with Source. So while of course you miss your dog, what you are really missing is the Connection to your own Source Energy that your dog inspired. . . .

- Your dog loved you as you are and did not ask you to be different.

- Your dog did not hold you responsible for his happiness.

- Your dog did enjoy being with you but never suffered in your absence, for his joy was not dependent upon your behavior.

- Your dog neither anticipated nor feared death, but understood the Eternal nature of his Being.

We cannot say any of these things about your father.

If we were standing in your physical shoes, we would focus upon the uplifted feeling that you so often felt in the company of your dog. Remember his eagerness to go with you for a walk. Remember his enthusiasm to chase a bird or a squirrel. Remember his peaceful demeanor as he lay on the floor with his head on his paws. And as you relax back into the good-feeling memory of the attitude of your dog, you will come back into alignment in the same way you used to when he was in the room with you. And then, if you like, the Universe will deliver another dog to replace him. If you are willing to do the work, you could attract a new puppy who will not chew on your shoes.

It is possible for you, in your understanding of vibration and of what your dog knew about alignment, to now achieve alignment and release the discomfort of missing your dog—and that is enough, for you may not feel the desire to co-create with another. In any case, we do not encourage getting another dog to try to fill the void of your last one, but, instead, to fill that void with what is really missing—alignment with your *Inner Being*—and then follow through with whatever action is inspired from that place of alignment.

Example 32

So, from your place of sadness, reach for better-feeling, *down-stream* thoughts:

> *Sometimes I forget for a minute that my dog isn't here, and then when I remember, I feel so sad.*
>
> *So many things around me make me think of him, and I miss him.*
>
> *I don't think that I'll ever be the same again now that he's gone.*
>
> *I've heard that time heals all wounds, but this isn't getting better.*
>
> *It hits me the hardest when I first come home and he isn't there to greet me.*

These statements are an accurate representation of how you are feeling and the kinds of thoughts you have been thinking about your dog. This process of reaching for slightly improved thoughts is designed to help you realize that while you cannot bring this wonderful dog back to life, you can feel better anyway, if you try. However, you cannot continue to think the same thoughts and say the same things and still find improvement. You have to reach for thoughts that feel better—so make the effort:

> *I'm not always sad, because I do focus on other things.*
>
> *Sometimes I go for quite a while without feeling the intense sadness about my dog.*
>
> *Even when my dog was alive, I didn't think about him all through the day.*
>
> *Often I was away from my house and without my dog.*

While these thoughts were easy to find from where you were just before, they feel significantly better than the last group of thoughts. Keep going:

> *I'm glad that I had the time I did with that wonderful dog.*
>
> *Someday I may find another dog that I'll love as well.*

When you find a thought (or a group of thoughts) that gives you a feeling of relief, it is helpful to stay with those thoughts for a while, repeating them and looking for thoughts that are similar to them. This process of reaching for *downstream* thoughts is not a race to see who can get the farthest *downstream* in the shortest amount of time, but simply about you finding a little bit of relief. If you will take the time to find the relieving statement and then acknowledge that you do, indeed, feel better, you will have accomplished a great deal.

I don't think I'm quite ready to get another dog.

A new puppy is a life-changing experience.

I remember my last dog when he was a puppy.

I threatened to take him back to where he came from nearly every day for weeks.

He always looked at me as if to say, <u>You don't really mean that.</u>

I would laugh and assure him that I didn't really mean that.

He was so much trouble in the beginning—and so much fun.

Now you may not be ready to go out and find another puppy, but you are feeling considerably better than just a few minutes ago. *We are not guiding you toward or away from bringing another dog into your life. This guidance is about you returning to your natural state of feeling good.*

It would be fun to get to know another dog.

Maybe I'll find one with a similar personality to my last dog.

I'll have to remember back to his puppy personality.

He was interested in everything . . . happy about everything.

I could use a little dose of that.

I think I'll think about that.

ᦔᦱᦰᦱᦰᦱ ᦰᦱᦰᦱᦰᦱ

Example 33

Our Son Is Gay

Example: "Our son left home for college last year, and when he came home for summer break recently, he told his father and me that he's gay and that he has met someone at school and has moved in with him.

"It's been a few weeks since his announcement, and while I'm feeling incredible sadness that our only son won't be giving us the gift of grandchildren, I've somewhat adjusted to it. But my husband is absolutely beside himself with anger. He's convinced that if my son hadn't gone to college and met this other boy, none of this would have happened. When I see how angry his father (who I know loves him very much) is, it terrifies me how my son will now be treated by the rest of the world."

It is never an easy thing for any parents to realize that their child has a different viewpoint on life—for most parents believe that through the hard work of their own life, they have come to the correct assumptions and conclusions about things, and then they work hard to pass these on to their own children.

If there could be only one thing that we could convince parents of—a thing that would help them to maintain a wonderful relationship with their children, a thing that would free parents and children from the pain of attempting the impossible—it would be this: *Your children are not you and did not come forth to be you. Your children came forth into this physical time-space reality with their own desires and plans.*

Your son being gay is not something that happened to him at college, and this is not a choice that he is making, here and now, from his physical point of view. This was something that was set into his Vibrational Escrow from his Non-Physical perspective before his physical birth.

We are often asked by people who define themselves as gay, "Why in the world would I choose something like this? Why would I choose to live a point of view so different from the majority of people who surround me? Why would I make a choice that causes me so much pain?" And we tell them:

> You did not specifically declare, from your Non-Physical vantage point, that you wanted to come forth into a physical body and be "gay," but you did have powerful intentions to come forth into this physical environment into a situation from which you could not be dissuaded. In other words, you knew that you were going to be born into an environment where you would be surrounded by others who believe that they have all the answers, who stand perched to pounce on you to convince you of the correctness of their beliefs.
>
> And from your broader Non-Physical vantage point, you intended, as you came forth into this body, to be different in a way that they would not understand, different in a way that they would want you to change, but different in a way that you *could not* change. In other words, it was your intention to help others understand the value of diversity and the impossible endeavor of demanding change from those who surround them. When you are willing to change in this way and in that way in order to help those around you feel better as they observe you, you do them a great disservice—for they never discover the freedom that only comes by understanding the power of their own thoughts.

Many people speak of unconditional love but rarely live it. Instead, when they see a condition that causes them to feel negative emotions, they demand a change in the condition; but in doing so,

Example 33

they set themselves on a long and uncomfortable path of attempting to control others in order to feel good.

When controlling others is necessary in order for you to feel good, you must confine yourself to a very small world over which you *can* gain control, and then you must give more time and energy than you possess to this impossible effort.

Unconditional love is just what it says: being connected to love and to *who-you-really-are,* regardless of the conditions. . . . "When I focus upon thoughts that my *Inner Being* agrees with, and therefore feel wonderful positive emotions, I'm in alignment with that which is love. My son, or anyone else, does not have to be different in order for me to remain connected to my Source of love."

And so, we would like you to understand that, with the most loving of intentions, your son has come forth to give you the gift of unconditional love. And there will be no greater joy in your lifetime than the embracing of this gift—and no greater pain than the refusing of it.

But you, sweet woman, have another two things to consider: (1) You have a son who is not pleasing your husband, and (2) you have a husband who is not pleasing *you.* We are not offering these words so that you can change the attitude of your husband toward your son or so that you can influence the behavior of your son. Your only power is in finding thoughts that your *Inner Being* agrees with and practicing them until they are the dominant thoughts within you.

It is our absolute promise to you that your *Inner Being* and the Source within you will never do other than adore your son no matter how many people condemn him. And when you are able to adore your husband, no matter what—or any others who may be unhappy about your son's sexuality—you will experience a freedom from resistance as you come into full alignment with *who-you-really-are* and with the Source within you.

So begin where you are, and try to make your way to the vantage point that your *Inner Being* holds about this:

My son is asking for so much grief in his life.

I wish, with all my heart, that he were not gay.

My husband is unbelievably stubborn, and I fear he'll never get over this.

It feels to me that our happy lives are all ruined, and I'm powerless to do anything about it.

My husband isn't even trying to understand.

My son can't help this, but my husband could be more understanding.

This isn't the only thing he's stubborn about, but this one matters more than the rest put together.

I hate that this has happened to us.

You have moved from powerlessness into anger and blame, so you are headed *downstream* in the direction of your *Inner Being*— but you still have a ways to go. Keep reaching for better-feeling thoughts:

This is all very new to us—in time we'll all get used to the idea.

It will not feel this awful forever.

My discomfort is much more about my husband's response to this than about the fact that my son is gay.

And my husband's response is probably more about how this could negatively affect our son rather than any condemnation of him.

This will all get better in time.

It will improve, especially since we all want to love one another.

Sometimes situations like this make you stronger as a family.

Nothing could ever happen to really break the bonds of love that we have for each other.

I'm going to relax in all this and stop reeling about in my own personal drama about it.

I can defuse it with my own more stable approach to it.

My husband is a reasonable man.

My husband is naturally a happy man.

Example 33

We are all happy people on a momentary sidetrack but we are on our way back to Well-Being.

This will be all right.

Now that you are closer to the way the Source within you feels about this, we will write the perspective of Source for you here. . . .

You are all extensions of Source Energy. You did not come forth into this physical experience with the intention of taking all of the ideas that exist and whittling them down to a handful of good ideas. You did not say, "I will go into the physical expression of life, figure out the right way to live on every subject, and then teach all others to live in that one perfect way." You understood that you were all coming forth with a variety of perspectives, orientations, and vantage points from which a steady stream of improved ideas would flow.

You were thrilled with the prospect of getting to explore the unending variety of ideas, situations, conditions, events, relationships, and all manner of things—for you understood that this variety would be the foundation from which your never-ending ideas of creativity would flow. And you knew that once a spark of desire shined brightly within you, the Source that is You would give its undivided attention to your newly expanded idea; and that that idea would then glisten off in the distance of your future, calling you toward it for the thrill of the ride.

You knew that you would never get it done and that you would never get it wrong . . . for, since it is never done, there is room for the Eternal alignment. And you knew, above all else, that the Source that is within you; the Source from which you have come; the Source who calls you forward; the Source whose gaze is never removed from you—the Source of *All-That-Is*—loves you unconditionally, now and forevermore!

There is great love here for you.

— **Abraham**

ᵉᖺ ᵉᖺ ᵉᖺ ᖷᵎ ᖷᵎ ᖷᵎ

Transcript of Abraham Live

Art of Allowing Workshop

(This *Art of Allowing* Workshop was recorded in Tampa, Florida, on Wednesday, November 1, 2006; and this live session is included as a free audio download [see page 263 for instructions] for your listening pleasure. [It has been edited slightly for clarity in these pages.] For additional tapes, CDs, books, videos, catalogs, or DVDs, or to reserve your space at an Abraham-Hicks *Art of Allowing* Workshop, please call [830] 755-2299; or write to Abraham-Hicks Publications at P.O. Box 690070, San Antonio, Texas 78269. Also, for an immediate overview of our works, visit our interactive Website at: **www.abraham-hicks.com**.)

Good morning. We are extremely pleased that you are here. It is good to come together for the purpose of co-creating, do you agree? Co-creating at its best, really. Are you enjoying your Leading Edge position here in your physical form? Are you appreciating the evolution of your desire? Are you finding that the contrast that you deliberately were born into is serving you well? Are you appreciating the contrast because of its life-giving quality?

We always poke and prod a little bit there, because often our physical friends are not that excited about the contrast in which they live. Many, especially when they realize that they came forth from a place of Pure, Positive Energy, sometimes say, "And why in the world would we project ourselves into an environment where there is so much that we don't want? What were we thinking?" And they often look around their environment and find things that they like, and they say, "Yes, I like that." But then they look around and they see things they don't like, and they say, "Oh no, I do not want that"—and then they resist that. They vote against it or push against it or find themselves feeling negative about it. And they often yearn for a different environment: "Let me find a relationship, or let me find a job, or let me find a home or a community or an environment where mostly only really good things happen. Because when I'm surrounded by really good things, I feel so much better than when there are bad things in the mix."

And we say, if you did not have the ability to focus, we could understand that concern. But since you are a focusing mechanism who has the ability to give your attention to what you choose, then we know that from your Broader Perspective, you would far rather have a buffet of choices than a buffet with no choices.

And you say, "Oh, but Abraham, you misunderstand. A buffet with only things I like to eat—what could possibly be wrong with that?"

And we say, you'd never find any improvement in what you eat. If you did not have the ability to evaluate contrast and to play what you want against what you don't want, you would not be able to come to new conclusions, which means the expansion of the Universe would cease. (Don't worry about it—it will never happen.)

You were wisely and deliberately born into an environment of enormous contrast. And from your Broader Non-Physical Perspective, you wanted that so much because you knew the value of it. So as we visit with our physical friends, we understand why when you haven't remembered that you have the ability to focus, and, even more, you haven't figured out how to guide your thoughts—in other words, when there's so much that you could think about and so much that's being projected through your airwaves and through your interaction with one another—we can understand how confusing it must be to try to sort out all of the possible things that you might think about. It must just drive you nuts.

But when you remember who you are and the vibrational stance from which you have come, you're going to remember that it is not only very easy to remain focused in the direction of that which you are, but that nothing else will do from your Broader

Perspective. It is the Eternal, inevitable nature of your Being to continue to expand—and you will and are. In fact, you can't stop that expansion, it is so assured.

So, we want to sort of give you a very brief version of the big picture to help you understand that you were Source Energy before you came into this physical body, and that you still are Source Energy even though you are now in this physical body. Now that's something that most humans don't really consciously acknowledge. They think, *Oh, I hope there was something before this; and, even more, I hope there will be something after this.* But few understand that you are Non-Physically and physically focused at the same time, and that both of those perspectives are active vibrations within you at all times. You're not dead *or* alive—in fact, you're never *dead.* You're always alive *and* Alive.

And so, you come forth from Non-Physical, focused into this physical body; and by your attention to different subjects, you activate vibrational frequencies within you. And the vibrational frequency that you activate as a result of what you're giving your attention to now is having vibrational feedback from the perspective of Source within you.

For example, when you look at yourself in the mirror and you feel contempt for yourself (you don't like yourself, you feel unworthy, you feel incapable, you feel guilty, you feel "not enough"), and you feel that negative emotion that you would call *unworthiness* or *guilt* or maybe even *self-blame*—when you feel those negative emotions—the reason that those emotions are present within you is because *your* now vantage point about you is so different from your *Source* vantage point about you.

When you look in the mirror and you feel proud of yourself or you feel eager about something, or you like yourself or you feel satisfaction with who you are, the reason that those feelings feel so good is because you're on the same vibrational wavelength with Source, who always adores you.

The same thing goes if you are looking at someone else. *Anytime you feel negative emotion—no matter what you call it or how extreme or soft it is—every time you feel negative emotion, it means one simple thing: You, in your human form, have deviated from the opinion of your Source.*

Now, that is a magnificent thing to understand because when you connect with that consciously, you have now activated in a real sense—in a real-time, moment-to-moment, conscious sense—your own *Guidance System*. You can always tell where you are, right now, in relationship with that Broader Perspective, and that is of enormous value to you because that Broader Perspective is the culmination of all that you have become. That Broader Perspective is the Eternal You in its most evolved form.

So back to the big picture: So you are *Source Energy,* and you project part of your attention into this physical body. And as you do so, now, in this physical body, you're having life experiences. You know what you *don't* want; you know what you *do* want, and all day, every day—whether you are speaking about it openly or not—you are launching rockets of desires, or preferences.

In other words, when someone is rude to you, you want them to be nicer, but when you're rude to someone, you want *yourself* to be nicer. When you don't feel good, you want to feel better. When you feel sick, you want to be well. When you don't have enough of something you want, you want to have it. In other words, life causes you to constantly give birth to new conclusions, and every one of you is doing it, even if you are a one-celled organism. And the expansion of all species—the expansion of everything that is—is as a result of that experience.

But here's the part that we think most humans have a hard time with (or at least have not yet done a very good job of getting their thoughts wrapped around): So you are Source Energy. You come forth into a physical body; and here, in this form, you give birth to new ideas. And this is the part we really want you to hear: Now the Source Energy part of you literally rides that rocket of your desire and *vibrationally* becomes whatever it is you are asking for.

Now this might not feel so meaningful to you because you're still looking at the manifestational world. You're looking around at the world that you *see*—which only exists because, at one time, it was *thought,* and then it became *thought-form* before it became the manifestation that you see.

So, when we tell you that the *Inner Being* part of you instantly becomes the *vibrational equivalent* of that which you are asking for, sometimes you don't feel all that excited about it. But if we were standing in your physical shoes, *we* would—because that's the beginning of the creation of whatever it is that you are asking for. In fact, it's such an important part of the story of creation and such an important part of how you create your own reality that we've written a book and given it the best title that we think has ever been given to a book: *Ask and It Is Given.* And the reason we like that title so much is because the title tells the whole story: *Ask and it is given.*

We wanted a longer title, but the publisher didn't think it was a good idea. We wanted the title to say: *So, I'm Non-Physical Energy, and I project part of that Consciousness into the physical form. And as I come into the physical form, the life experience that I'm living causes me to constantly weigh the pros and the cons of what I'm living and to give birth to constant rockets of desires. And when that happens, the Non-Physical part of me not only answers what I'm asking for—not only gives me what I'm asking for—but literally <u>becomes</u> the vibrational equivalent of that which I am asking for.* They said it was too long, but *Ask and It Is Given* tells you the same thing.

When life causes you to ask, Source not only *gives* it, but *becomes* it. Now, if you just heard that, then you have just found the key to the *Guidance* within you, because these two points of vibrational relativity will help you always know whether or not you're on the same wavelength of that which is Source. And this is particularly important when you remember what we just said: Your life caused you to want *more* of *this,* to want an *improvement* of *this.* In other words, you have incrementally been building *this* picture of your life experience, even before you came into this physical body (and emphatically ever since) so that you have created this powerful Leading Edge Beingness that already exists. And Source stands there, being it, pulsing it; and the *Law of Attraction* is responding to that vibrational state of Being. (Did you get that?) That means, as the *Law of Attraction* is summoning that expanded version of you, talk about *Life Force!* Talk about *inspiration!* Talk about the *Stream of Life!* Talk about the *call of Source!* In other words, are you getting a sense of why you feel compelled or inspired to move in the direction you do? It's because life has caused you—through what you're living—to literally expand and become more; and that expanded version of you now must *be.*

Many of you have to croak before you *let* it be. We like that word, *croak.* (We try to be as disrespectful as we can about the idea of "death," since there isn't any.) Sometimes your life causes you to be this expanded version of you, but instead of letting yourself go to where you want to be, you beat the drum of *what-is,* and so you hold yourself apart from your expansion—and you feel terrible while you do it. But then when you die, the gap closes. So, what we're wanting you to remember is that, oh, there is no such thing as death, but when you have that experience that you *call* death, you release your habits of thought, which are the only things that are hindering you from being what life has caused you to become.

So, we call this gathering the *Art of Allowing,* and it really is the art of closing that gap. "It's the art of allowing myself, in my physical human form, to be what life has caused me to become. It's the art of releasing resistance and allowing the Energy that creates worlds to flow through me. It's the art of coming into vibrational alignment, not only with who I was before I was born, but with who I've become since. It is the art of coming into vibrational alignment with the Pure, Positive Energy Being that I am constantly in the state of becoming." (You get this?)

So, when you have feelings of unfulfillment—when you feel not enough, when you feel dissatisfied—that means you're just not letting yourself get up to speed with You.

So now you've heard this story of who you are. And now we want you to get the fuller sense that *this story of the cycle of life represents you from Non-Physical coming into physical, giving birth to new thoughts that the Non-Physical part of you becomes.* As you begin to understand this cycle of life that the *Law of Attraction* is at the heart of, then you begin to understand the Eternal nature of your Being.

We are all Eternal Beings, and you are on the Leading Edge, giving birth to new expansion—and Source immediately becomes it. (How good is that?) Well, we say, from our vantage point, it is magnificent. And from your vantage point, when you let yourself be up to speed with it, you think it is magnificent, too. But when life causes you to be something that you don't (for whatever reason) let yourself be, then it beats up on you pretty good.

Imagine taking your canoe down to the river's edge and putting it in the very fast-moving river. And you have your oars inside, and you deliberately point your canoe *upstream* and begin paddling very hard *against* the current. And we say, why not turn and go *with* the current? Why not turn and go *with* the flow?

And most humans say, "To tell you the truth, it never entered my mind because everyone I know who wants to amount to anything is trying harder than that. That just seems lazy." (Fun)

"And so, I have positioned myself," you say. "I have a really good boat. I have really good oars. See how they're hooked onto the edge there? I have moleskin on my hands. And I have muscles. And, even more, I have determination. . . . And I learned it from my mother (Fun), who learned it from her mother. It's what we all do. We try harder."

And we say, *But how long can you keep it up?*

And you say, "Till death do us part. You see, I don't know how long, but all of the rewards, Abraham, all of the rewards and statues and monuments are given to those who really try hard. (Fun) And I want some of those." And then you often remind us that you have heard that there are even more rewards after you die for those who really try hard. (Fun)

So, you work hard to convince us of the appropriateness of paddling *against* the current, and we always listen lovingly, because we understand your perspective. But then we have to eventually stop you and say to you something that we want (with everything that we are) for you to hear: <u>*Nothing that you want is upstream. Not one thing that you want is* upstream.</u>

And do you know how we know that? We know the cycle. We know who you were before you were born. We know what your life has caused you to do in the launching of rockets of desire. We know that the Source within you has become the vibrational equivalent of what you're asking for, and we know that the *Law of Attraction* is responding to that powerful, pulsing vibration; and we know that that's what causes the Current.

A woman said to us, not long ago (she went to lunch with her children and came back to the seminar, and she was the first one that we called to the chair to ask a question) . . . she said, "My child asked me to ask you a question: 'Why are grown-ups so grumpy?'" And we said, because the longer you live, the more you find to fuss and worry about. The longer you live, the more you find things you do not want and the more things you shout *no* at; and the more things you shout *no* at, the more you turn *against* the Current.

Jerry and Esther had the delightful experience a few weeks ago of going white-water rafting on a wonderful river in Colorado. It was a very fast-moving river; it was classed as IV rapids, so it was a really moving river. And as they were approaching the river—as they were driving alongside the river in the bus with all of the others, with the boats on top, up the canyon—Jerry and Esther looked at this river and said to one another, more than once, "We must be out of our minds."

It was a raging river. The water was spiking high over some of the big boulders and around the bridges and such, and as they put their raft into the water . . . (They were with friends, six of them went together, and then there were many other rafts, that were with the same river company, who were all high-school wrestling teams. Their friend who had invited them on this trip, her daughter said to him as he left the house that morning, "Did you tell them how old you all are?") . . . as they put their boat into the water, it was evident to them right away that there was no value whatsoever in attempting to paddle *upstream*. It did not even enter their minds because they could see that that river was going to have its way with them.

The man who was teaching them what to do, who was the guide in their raft, said to them, "Friends, this is not Disneyland, and we cannot turn this river off." And the reason that he was telling them that is because he knows the power of the river. He knows the force of the river. He pointed out big rock pilings, and he said to them, "We don't want our raft to get wedged in those rocks because if that happens, the river will just beat us up." And then he referred them to page 5, paragraph 3, of the disclaimer they had signed, which made it absolutely obvious that the likelihood of their survival was almost none. (Fun) Esther refused to read it. She read the first paragraph and said, "I take your word for it."

The reason that we are giving this to you in this way is because we want you to understand that *your* river is like that. You can't turn it off. Your river was flowing before you even came forth into this physical body, and the longer you live, the faster it flows, because every time you live an experience, you ask for something more. And every time you ask for something more, Source becomes it. And every time the Source part of you becomes it, *Law of Attraction* responds to it. And every time *Law of Attraction* responds to the you (that is in the process of becoming), your Stream moves faster.

You could have the same negative thoughts that you developed when you were 4 or 5 or 10 or 15 or 20—you could have the same negative attitude about something; it doesn't need to have changed at all—but 10 or 15 or 20 or 30 or 40 or 50 or 60 years later, that negative attitude that hasn't changed at all is taking a much greater toll on you because your Stream's moving faster. And the *Law of Attraction* says it can't stand still; it is changing. So, if you've been beating the drum of something that you don't want, then that *vibration* within you is getting stronger and stronger at the same time your *asking* is getting stronger and stronger.

So, you're causing your Stream to go faster, in that example, and you are also refusing to go with the Stream. That's what *negative emotion* is; that's what *negative sensation* is—that's what *dis-ease* is.

Even children who get sick are experiencing sickness because their life is causing them to want something that they don't believe they can have. In other words, when you have that powerless, out-of-control feeling, and something really matters to you, but you have a belief that says, *I can't get what I want to get,* you put yourself in this impossible position, because there is a tug-of-war going on within you, Energy-wise, that does not serve you well.

Now the good news is: *It doesn't matter where you are. At any point, you can turn and go with the flow—at any point. In fact, you don't even have to turn and row with the flow. Just let go of the oars . . . the Stream will turn you.*

Sometimes you listen to us as we crow about all of these good-feeling emotions: *appreciation* and *love* and *joy* and *passion,* and all of that good-feeling stuff up here. And it makes you think that, under all conditions and at all costs, you should turn your boat around, *trrrrrr,* put a motor on it and get down there to the good-feeling emotion as fast as you can.

And we say, we want you to get down there where it feels better and better, but because we know the power of the Stream, there is no urgency about your getting down there. *We know, if you'll just stop doing that thing you do that's got you pointing <u>against</u> the Current, that the Current will turn you and take you.*

We also know that you don't have a choice. You can't be down there because something has happened (something's happened to someone you love or something's happening in your own life experience . . . you want something, you can't figure out how to get it, you're depressed or feeling enraged or angry or any negative emotion; doesn't matter what you call it—fear), you can't, in your state of negative emotion, all of a sudden just turn your boat around and speed right down there to where it feels good. You can't do that. And you don't have to do that. *All you have to do is stop paddling upstream—and the Stream will carry you.*

So, we want to leave you with a very keen awareness of the emotion that you're most wanting to reach for (we call them all kinds of things from *despair* and *grief* and *fear,* into *revenge* and *rage* and *anger,* into *frustration* and *overwhelment,* into *pessimism,* into *hopefulness,* into *optimism,* into *believing,* into *knowing,* into *love,* into *joy*). And there are so many other words that could be applied somewhere along that *Emotional Scale,* but there's only one word that is necessary for you to apply to your emotional state of Being. This is the emotion that we want you to reach for all day, every day, no matter where you put your boat in: *It's the emotion of relief.*

When you feel *despair* or *fear* (they feel so much the same), and you reach for something that feels less awful and you find *revenge*— you now *feel relief.* People don't want to hear that, especially those who live with you. They liked you better when you were depressed. You were less trouble. (Fun) But if you've ever been *afraid* or in *despair,* and you found the breath of fresh air that *revenge* gave you, you know you *felt relief.*

Now we're not encouraging you to stand there and beat the drum of revenge, because as the Stream continues to move, *revenge* will be *upstream* soon. (Isn't that an interesting thought?) So, you're in *despair.* You let go of the thought that's causing it, and the Stream turns you and now you *feel relief.* But if you don't keep turning to go with the flow, if you keep turning back, this Stream is going to continue to ask you to turn and turn and turn and turn, and turn. So, when you turn from *revenge* into *anger,* you *feel relief* again; and when you turn from *anger* into *frustration,* you *feel relief* again; and when you turn from *frustration* into *hoping,* you *feel* relief again. (You get the sense of this?)

So, let your intention be *not* to turn and try to paddle *downstream, because when you've got something that you're trying to make happen and you don't know how to make it happen, and you get hold of those oars and try to paddle downstream—you always turn and go upstream.*

People try to effect a "healing"—they always turn *upstream.* They try to make something "better" happen—*they turn upstream.* They say, "I'm going to set a goal"—they turn and go *upstream,* because there's something in the attitude of *trying* that always makes you turn *against* the current. It's something very different when you just let go: You call it surrendering. We don't call it giving up on your desires . . . you can't—*your desires are Eternal.* You cannot become less than you have become. You can't live life, which causes you to ask for more, and then say, "Never mind." You can't do that. You can continue to amend your desire, but you continue to expand, and your Stream continues to go faster, and (we love you very much, but) *you have no choice but to go with the flow if you are wanting to feel good.*

It's always so exhilarating to watch one of you croak, because when you croak, you let go of those oars. And, oh, what a ride on the river that is, that immediate reemergence into Pure, Positive Energy and into the full becoming of what life has caused you to become. We're just here visiting with you because we think it would be great fun for you to catch up with *who-you-are* while you're still here in this physical body. Future generations will benefit by that which you are living. In other words, the contrast that you live as you see the war and want it not; as you want Well-Being; as you see people hungry and you want them to be fed; as you live what's happening in your neighborhood, in your country, or in your world, or in your household—as you live it, you give constant birth to rockets of desire, and you and your life experience are in an Eternal state of becoming. And here's the thing that most of you have not considered: That state is the vibrational stance from which you are then born into this physical experience. (Do you get that?)

That's why the babies that are being born are cable ready. (Fun) That's why they understand the Internet; that's why they get the new contraptions. They were born from the Leading Edge Energy of all of that. They are resistance free. That's what the "generation gap" is about. It's not a generation gap; it's an Energy gap . . . it's a resistance gap. And so, the *Art of Allowing* is really about you figuring out how to keep up with You. And when you allow yourself to keep up with You, oh, what an exhilarating life it is!

Can you imagine Jerry and Esther saying to their river guide, "Where will we take the boat out of the water?"

And he would say, "Oh, many miles downstream, close to Fort Collins."

And then Esther would say to him, "Well, we have a really good idea: We want you to put our raft back on the bus, and we would like to *drive* back down. And we want to put our boat in the water just a few hundred feet from where we were going to take it out—because we enjoy *instant* manifestations."

And he would say, "Whatever you want, crazy lady (Fun), but I thought you wanted a ride on the river."

And this is what we want to say to you: *We thought you wanted a ride on the river.* And you say, "I do want a ride on the river, but I just don't want to be without what I want for 10 or 20 or 30 or 40 or 50 years. How long does one have to want something before they get it?" And we say, hardly any time at all if you're going with the flow. Forever, if you're not.

Not "forever," just forever in terms of this one life experience. In other words, you could hold yourself apart from who you have become if you work really hard at it. You have to join those online support groups (Fun), however; you have to join those groups who really keep you motivated about not letting go of the oars. . . . When you sleep, you know what happens? Your boat turns around . . . *ahhh.* Then you wake up and you paddle, paddle, paddle, paddle. Then you go to sleep . . . *ahhh.* You wake up, paddle, paddle, paddle, paddle. (Fun)

So what happens is, you are Pure, Positive Energy. You are one Stream, and then you are born into that little infant body. And just being born to that mother who worried about you already, there's a little separation in your vibration. And when you go to sleep, you close the gap. When you wake up, it's there just a little bit. And the longer you live, most of you, the more you find to fuss and worry about, and the more likely you are to have more of a gap between letting yourself be and *who-you-really-are.*

Then you grow up, and you want to improve your life experience. And so, you come to a seminar where they teach you to meditate. You learn to quiet your mind; and when you quiet your mind, you stop thought; and when you stop thought, you stop *resistant* thought—so your gap closes. . . . Then you come out of meditation; you find someone to criticize—you widen your gap. You find someone to praise—you close it. You look for things going wrong—you widen it. You look for things going well—you close it. In other words, a *Rampage of Appreciation* always closes your gap, and looking for things that are wrong always widens your gap. So, all day, every day, you've got this thing going on, depending upon what you're doing with your thought process.

The *Art of Allowing* is really about paying attention to the way you feel—so that you are aware of this gap between you and You— and guiding yourself deliberately to less-resistant thoughts just by releasing the thought that is negative. You really don't even have to get on a really strong positive rampage—just stop talking about the things that are bothering you so much.

Jerry and Esther drive a big bus. It's 45 feet long, and Esther is usually driving, and Jerry is in the back somewhere doing something—often he is working on some project or watching a video or viewing something. Often he is far in the back of the bus, and Esther sometimes will want to talk to him, and so she used to honk the horn. But even honking the horn, he couldn't hear her sometimes; it was scaring everyone on the road off into the bushes (Fun), but Jerry couldn't hear it because he had his headphones on, or whatever.

And so, Esther found a button next to her that she could push; and when she pushes the button, *all* the lights in the bus come on. And when she pushes it again, *all* the lights in the bus go off. And so, when Jerry sees the lights coming on and the lights going off, he surmises, "Oh, Esther must have something she wants to say."

So he stows everything that he's working on, and he makes his way all the way to the front of the bus. And he sits in the seat next to her, and he says, "Yes, you had something you wanted to say?" And Esther says, "Oh, never mind. It was an *upstream* thought." (Fun)

Wasn't it nice that it took him so long to get there? Because if he'd been sitting there right next to her, she just would have blurted it out. And then he might have agreed with her, which would have made it worse. Or he might have disagreed with her, which would have made her try even harder to make her point. In other words, once you speak your discord, someone either agrees with you, which amplifies it, or they disagree with you, which makes you get stronger in your certainty that what you have to say is right. In other words, when you speak anything that's already pointed *upstream*, you're going to paddle harder and stronger, but when you stop for a moment and count to ten and identify, *Is this an <u>upstream</u> thought or a <u>downstream</u> thought? Is this a thought that my <u>Inner Being</u> is thinking about? Hmm, no, it doesn't really feel like that. Is this a thought that my <u>Inner Being</u> is more in agreement with?* in time you begin to notice that you can always *feel* that calling of Source. You can feel it if you will listen for it. It takes a little practice, and it takes a little practice on subject after subject. But before you know it, you will become so sensitive to the vibration of your Being that you will be able to use this *Guidance* in the way that you intended it.

Instead of trying to sort out every thought in the world or every thought you've ever thought—or all the thoughts of all the people in a room or of the people on your bus or the people in your community or in your political party or in your church or in the world—instead of trying to sort out all those thoughts, which just makes you crazy, *you can <u>feel</u> what your <u>Inner Being</u> knows about everything. You can <u>feel</u> what you have become. And when you reach for that <u>feeling</u>—and you move in the direction of it—you feel the ease of your body.*

In the moment that you let go of those oars, the majority of the resistance subsides (even though it might take you a while to float downstream to the manifestation of what you want). In the moment you let go of those oars, the majority of the illness, if there is illness in your body, subsides. (We're not kidding you.) *Relief is the cure that all medicine is looking for.* Rather than looking for the *cure,* look for the vibrational cause. You don't even have to find the cause. You don't even have to find the thought that *is* causing the resistance—you just have to find a thought that *isn't* causing resistance.

You don't have to sort it all out. You don't have to go back and retrace your steps through it and figure out which way you went wrong. You just have to reach for a thought of <u>relief.</u>

The other day, Jerry and Esther were leaving Orlando on their way to Boca Raton, and Esther programmed the navigational system in the car. And all of a sudden, Jerry says, "It feels to me that we are going in the wrong direction."

And Esther looked at the screen, and she said, "I'm doing everything that it said."

And Jerry said, "This *can't* be right."

And Esther said, "Well, let's just play it out and see where it takes us."

And so it took them on the tollway going what Jerry considered to be the wrong direction. Then it had them exit onto Interstate 4, continue a short distance, make a U-turn, and get back on the tollway and go the other way. It was about a ten-minute diversion from where they needed to be. And Jerry is laughing, because it was clear to him that that was what was happening—and what a funny thing.

And then Esther said, "I wonder if the machine is just nuts, or if I misunderstood and took the wrong entrance and then it repro-grammed itself so quickly to say, 'Well, now that you're here, *this* is the best way to go.'"

And so, now Esther is really curious. "Was the navigational system the crazy lady, or was *I* the crazy lady?" And she said to Jerry, "You know what would be really fun? We could just go back and start over and retrace our steps and figure out where we went wrong."

And Jerry said, "Or we could just keep going right." (Fun)

What a novel idea. You mean, start from where I am? You mean, not go back and figure out what went wrong? You mean, not go back and place blame or figure out who was the wrong one—just start where I am? And we say, that really *is* what we wish for you.

You put your boat in the river wherever you put your boat in the river, and you know what? <u>*You are* where you *are.*</u> A very good mantra: *I am where I am.* And another good mantra: *I am where I am—and it's okay.* Not only is it *okay,* not only is it *enough, it's <u>got to be okay</u> because it's all you've got.* In other words, you've got no choice, so it might be a good one to make peace with: *I am where I am.* (Oh, that *is* making peace, isn't it?)

"I am where I am—and it's okay." And why is it okay?

"Because I am where I am—and that's okay." And why is it okay?

"Because I have no choice—so it *has* to be okay. *I have no choice: I am where I am.*

"I am where I am. I've put my boat in the river at *sickness,* or I've put my boat in the river at *wellness.* I've put my boat in the river at *abundance,* or I've put my boat in the river at *not enough* of something. I've put my boat in the river in the middle of a *divorce* or a *horrible experience,* or I've put my boat in the river in the middle of *love.* . . . I've put my boat in the river, but wherever I've put my boat in the river, on whatever subject is active within me, *I am where I am—and it's okay. And it's got to be okay, because it's enough."* This is going to take a while. (Fun)

We'd like to stay here all day, because we want you to say: "I am where I am—and it's enough. And I am where I am—and it's enough. And there's only one emotion that matters, and that's the emotion of *relief.* In other words, right now *I am where I am—and it's okay because it's all I've got.* I do have a powerful, fabulous choice: *downstream* or *upstream!*

"Feeling a little better, feeling a little worse: That's all I've got—but it's enough, because if wherever I am, I'd reach for the *downstream* thought, and *now* wherever I am, I reach for the *downstream* thought, and *now* wherever I am, I reach for the *downstream* thought, and *now,* wherever I am—no matter what's happening—I reach for the *downstream* thought. . . ." You know what happens? You begin to go with the flow.

As you begin to go with the flow, since everything that you want is downstream, you begin to float into desired circumstances and events. All kinds of things that you've been waiting for—sometimes for a long time—become almost immediately apparent to you, because the only thing that was keeping you from them was that you were paddling upstream.

And do you know what's really interesting, from our aerial view, from which we see everything? (This is one of the things that when you croak will amuse you most of all. At least, that's what we hear from recent croakers.) The Stream is so magnificent that it inevitably carries you to everything that you want—eventually. And the faster you turn willingly and go with it, the faster you receive it.

Many of you have your back to *downstream;* your nose is pointing *upstream;* and you're paddling so hard that even though you're strong enough, the Stream of Well-Being is so strong that it's taking you downstream toward what you want anyway. You don't see it. You float right by it. You miss your opportunities because you're not a Vibrational Match to them, so you don't see them—where if you're in this relaxed state of trusting and expecting, it's so much easier. (You have a very good picture of that, don't you?)

You are powerful creators who have come here with great reason, and you are so much more than you see here in these physical bodies. And when you allow yourself to relax a little from where you are and turn and go with the flow, you are going to discover —in your first day of making a decision about that—the power of this Stream. *You're going to discover the power of the Stream and the power of the <u>Law of Attraction</u> and the power of your worthiness—and the Eternal nature of your Being.*

Life is supposed to be good for you. It is supposed to *feel* good. It is supposed to *feel* fun. *Life is supposed to feel good to you.*

You never came forth for the struggle, but you *did* come forth for the contrast, because the contrast gives birth to the power of the Stream. The contrast puts what you want in Vibrational Escrow. The contrast causes the expansion of your Being.

"So, how can I be in my physical body and benefit by the contrast and still become the Being that life causes me to be? . . . By being alert and awake and by not being afraid of what comes—by taking it in and by seeing what I *don't* want and knowing what I *do* want, and then by caring so much about how I feel that I'm always reaching for the best-feeling thought that I can find."

And before you know it, the contrast of your life will not be this raging contrast. When you *really* know what you *don't* want, you *really* know what you *do* want—but you're far apart. So the more you turn and go with the flow, what begins to happen to you is, your contrast becomes less exaggerated.

Now, for those of you who like the drama of it, you might not want to go this softer way. But you can reach the place where contrast says, *I'd like that.* You go with the flow and you receive it. *I'd like that.* You go with the flow and you receive it. *I'd like that. . . .*

So, you want it; you *get* it. You want it; you *get* it. You want it; you *get* it. (We could go on.) But the way *you* often play it is: You want it; you don't have it. You want it; you don't have it. You want it; you don't have it.

"I don't have it. I don't have it. I don't have it. I don't have it. *You* don't have it, either. You don't have it. You don't have it. You don't have it. I don't have it. I see *you* don't have it. How do *you* like not having it? You don't like it, either? I don't like not having it. *They've* got it; we don't have it. We don't have it. We should join the group *Those Against Not Having It—Those Against Not Having What*

We Want." And the more you don't have it, the more you want it. And the more you talk about not having it, the more you want it. So, you get your Stream moving faster and faster, and faster.

Then you say, "You know, I don't really feel that good." And we say, that's because your life has caused you to get this rip-roaring Stream going, and you're joining these groups that aren't going with the Stream, and you're tearing yourself apart.

And you say, "I know—I saw the x-ray. . . . I know—I got the blood test." And we say, just let go. Just let go of whatever it is that doesn't feel good—and you'll begin going with the flow.

Do you know that you're not sick because you think specifically of sickness? Once you're sick, you *stay* sick because you think of the sickness, but you're not sick *because* you think of sickness. You're sick because you don't like that man at work. You're sick because you feel unfulfilled. You're sick because someone disagreed with you and betrayed you 25 years ago, and you've talked about it every day since. You're sick because you're beating the drum of unwanted stuff—because this isn't Disneyland—and no one can turn off the Stream. You don't want it to be turned off—it's the call of *Life;* it's the call of *Source,* you see.

It is our desire to assist you, wherever you are, in just turning and going with the flow. We'll give you every trick in our bag of tricks to help you release the resistance that is the only thing that is keeping you from what you want. And so, if it is your desire to find improvement in your gap between where you are, on any subject, and where you want to be, we are eager to visit with you.

For every question you have, we have an answer. For every problem, there is a solution. For every misunderstanding, there is understanding. For every confusion, there is clarity . . . not because we hold a magic bag, but because we know the *Laws,* we know your inevitable nature, we know the power of the *Stream*—and we have seen your future.

You know what to do, don't you? You know that you're the creator of your own experience, yes? You know that you are *Source Energy* in a physical body . . . you do, don't you? You know that you have come here to be in this Leading Edge environment for the thrill of expansion, yes? And you can *feel* that you are definitely expanding? Can't you *feel* this Vibrational Escrow that is the becoming of you? And haven't you gathered, from this conversation, that that part of you is as real as it will be once it manifests?

That's the part that we so much want you to hear: *We want you to know that the question that you hold has been answered—you've just got to let yourself flow toward the answer. We want you to know that the dilemma that you feel faced with has been solved—you just have to let yourself flow toward the solution. You just have to not struggle in the interim. You just have to trust that the power of the Stream and the worthiness of your Being is enough—because it is.*

Don't you just love knowing that you have come forth into this Leading Edge environment with the specific intent of letting life cause you to be more? And don't you find it humorous? (We do.) Don't you find it humorous? (You will when you croak.) But you find all of these things to fuss and worry about and use them as your reason to not let yourself go with that which you have become.

A friend said to us, "Abraham, I don't think you care if my lover ever comes. I think you just want me to get so good at visualizing him that I now no longer notice that he isn't here." And we said, *That is exactly right. Because when you get so good at visualizing him that you don't feel pain about him not being there now, you're in align-ment with your own dream, and he has to come—but until you come into alignment with your own dream, there is not enough action in the world to make any difference.*

It will feel to you, when you're not in alignment, as if not only is the world not cooperating with you, but the world is deliberately against you. But when you come into alignment with *who-you-are,* you will come to feel that nothing can keep you from anything that you want. There are no adverse forces. There are no contradictory intentions. There are no others in competition. There is nothing that can deprive you of that which you want to be or do, or have— nothing can deprive you other than your attention to the absence of what you want.

Your work isn't to convince someone to give you something you want; your work is to just find relief from wherever you are. When you get good at finding relief, you'll begin to flow with your Stream, and these things that have been *downstream* waiting for you to queue up with them will begin to connect with you with such extraordinary persistence that people who are watching you will wonder what in the world has happened with you.

They will begin to describe you as those who barely begin to speak what they want and it seems that Heaven and Earth begin moving toward the fulfillment of it. They will describe you as those who, no matter what is happening, are always able to maintain their emotional balance. They will describe you as those who are always optimistic, even in pessimistic circumstances. They might even call you "Pollyanna," but what they will definitely begin to notice about you is that your life is working in extraordinary ways.

And as they watch in amazement at the remarkable things that they have known you've wanted for years that now are beginning to flow into your experience, along with things that they just heard you identify last week that are already flowing into your experience, they'll say, "What in the world is going on with you?"

And you will explain to them, "There is this Stream. . . . (Fun) And I finally got an awareness of it, and I've stopped battling the Current of my own intentions. I finally came into alignment with *me*."

They will say, "So does that mean that everything you want is in place?"

And you'll say, "Oh no, far from that, because every day I dream new dreams."

And they'll say, "Oh, so you're not really fulfilled and completed?"

And you say, "Hardly—I never will be. But I was not born to get stuff done. I was born to dream it and then move toward it. I didn't come to *manifest* a woman. I came to *want* her; it feels so good to want her. It feels so good to want her and so bad to believe I can't have her, but *wanting* her is what I really wanted. *Finding* her will be delicious, too, but there is so much deliciousness in the wanting." *Wanting* in *belief* is *life-giving*. *Wanting* in *doubt* is horrible. And now you know that you have the choice.

We are exhilarated about what's *downstream* for you. We've seen it—it's good. It's going to knock your socks off when you allow yourself to float in the direction of it—at first. But by the time it's ready to manifest, it will feel so much like the next logical step that you'll say, "Oh, there you are. I knew you were there. I could feel you."

There is great love here for you.
And, for now, as always,
we remain eternally and happily incomplete.

⋘ ⋘ ⋘ ⋙ ⋙ ⋙

About the Authors

Excited about the clarity and practicality of the translated word from the Beings who call themselves Abraham, **Esther** and **Jerry Hicks** began disclosing their amazing Abraham experience to a handful of close business associates in 1986.

Recognizing the practical results being received by themselves and by those people who were asking practical questions and then applying Abraham's answers to their own situations, Esther and Jerry made a deliberate decision to allow the teachings of Abraham to become available to an ever-widening circle of seekers of how to live a happier life.

Using their San Antonio, Texas, conference center as their base, Jerry and Esther have traveled to approximately 50 cities a year since 1989, presenting interactive *Law of Attraction* workshops to those leaders who gather to participate in this expanding stream of progressive thought. And although worldwide attention has been given to this philosophy of Well-Being by Leading Edge thinkers and teachers who have, in turn, incorporated many of Abraham's *Law of Attraction* concepts into their best-selling books, scripts, lectures, and so forth, the primary spread of this material has been from person to person—as individuals begin to discover the value of this form of spiritual practicality in their personal life experiences.

In November 2011, Jerry made his transition into Non-Physical, and now Esther continues to conduct the Abraham workshops with the help of her physical friends and co-workers and, of course, with the Non-Physical help of Abraham and Jerry.

People are able to access Abraham directly by attending the seminars in person or by participating in the online live streaming of most events. There is also an extensive YouTube library of Abraham videos.

Abraham—a group of uplifting Non-Physical teachers—present their Broader Perspective through Esther Hicks. And as they speak to our level of comprehension through a series of loving, allowing, brilliant, yet comprehensively simple essays in print and in sound, they guide us to a clear connection with our loving *Inner Being,* and to uplifting self-empowerment from our Total Self.

Abraham-Hicks Publications may be contacted through the extensive interactive website: **www.abraham-hicks.com**; or by mail at Abraham-Hicks Publications, P.O. Box 690070, San Antonio, TX 78269.

Bonus Content

Thank you for purchasing *The Astonishing Power of Emotions* by Esther and Jerry Hicks (The Teachings of Abraham®). This product includes a free download! To access this bonus content, please visit www.hayhouse.com/download and enter the Product ID and Download Code as they appear below.

Product ID: 3721
Download Code: ebook

For further assistance, please contact
Hay House Customer Care by phone:
US (800) 654-5126 or INTL CC+(760) 431-7695
or visit www.hayhouse.com/contact.php

Thank you again for your Hay House purchase. Enjoy!
Hay House, Inc. • P.O. Box 5100 • Carlsbad, CA 92018
(800) 654-5126

Publisher's note: Hay House products are intended to be powerful, inspirational, and life-changing tools for personal growth and healing. They are not intended as a substitute for medical care. Please use this audio program under the supervision of your care provider. Neither the author nor Hay House, Inc., assumes any responsibility for your improper use of this product.

NOTES

NOTES

Hay House Titles of Related Interest

-∘[🖾]∘-

All of the above are available at your local bookstore,
or may be ordered by contacting Hay House (see next page).

-∘[🖾]∘-